SAT CollegeBoard

FROM THE MAKER OF THE TEST

The Official SAT Subject Test Study Guide

Chemistry

The College Board
New York, N.Y.

About the College Board

The College Board is a mission-driven not-for-profit organization that connects students to college success and opportunity. Founded in 1900, the College Board was created to expand access to higher education. Today, the membership association is made up of over 6,000 of the world's leading educational institutions and is dedicated to promoting excellence and equity in education. Each year, the College Board helps more than seven million students prepare for a successful transition to college through programs and services in college readiness and college success—including the SAT® and the Advanced Placement Program®. The organization also serves the education community through research and advocacy on behalf of students, educators, and schools.

For further information, visit collegeboard.org.

Copies of this book are available from your bookseller or may be ordered from College Board Publications at store.collegeboard.org or by calling 800-323-7155.

Editorial inquiries concerning this book should be addressed to the College Board, SAT Program, 250 Vesey Street, New York, New York 10281.

ISBN 13: 978-1-4573-0919-9

Printed in the United States of America

3 4 5 6 7 8 9   23 22 21 20 19 18 17

Distributed by Macmillan

Contents

The SAT Subject Tests™

About SAT Subject Tests

SAT Subject Tests™ are a valuable way to help you show colleges a more complete picture of your academic background and interests. Each year, nearly one million Subject Tests are taken by students throughout the country and around the world to gain admission to the leading colleges and universities in the United States.

SAT Subject Tests are one-hour exams that give you the opportunity to demonstrate knowledge and showcase achievement in specific subjects. They provide a fair and reliable measure of your achievement in high school — information that can help enhance your college admission portfolio. The Chemistry Subject Test is a great way to highlight your understanding, skills, and strengths in chemistry.

This book provides information and guidance to help you study for and familiarize yourself with the Chemistry Subject Test. It contains actual, previously administered tests and official answer sheets that will help you get comfortable with the tests' format, so you feel better prepared on test day.

The Benefits of SAT Subject Tests

SAT Subject Tests let you to put your best foot forward, allowing you to focus on subjects that you know well and enjoy. They can help you differentiate yourself in a competitive admission environment by providing additional information about your skills and knowledge of particular subjects. Many colleges also use Subject Tests for course placement and selection; some schools allow you to place out of introductory courses by taking certain Subject Tests.

Subject Tests are flexible and can be tailored to your strengths and areas of interest. These are the **only** national admission tests where **you** choose the tests that best showcase your achievements and interests. You select the Subject Test(s) and can take up to three tests in one sitting. With the exception of listening tests, you can even decide to change the subject or number of tests you want to take on the day of the test. This flexibility can help you be more relaxed on test day.

REMEMBER
Subject Tests are a valuable way to help you show colleges a more complete picture of your academic achievements.

Who Should Consider Subject Tests?

Anyone can take an SAT Subject Test to highlight his or her knowledge of a specific subject. SAT Subject Tests may be especially beneficial for certain students:

- Students applying to colleges that require or recommend Subject Tests — be aware that some schools have additional Subject Test requirements for certain students, majors, or programs of study

- Students who wish to demonstrate strength in specific subject areas

- Students who wish to demonstrate knowledge obtained outside a traditional classroom environment (e.g., summer enrichment, distance learning, weekend study, etc.)

- Students looking to place out of certain classes in college

- Students enrolled in dual-enrollment programs

- Home-schooled students or students taking courses online

- Students who feel that their course grade may not be a true reflection of their knowledge of the subject matter

The SAT Subject Test in Chemistry is particularly useful for students interested in majors with a focus in STEM (Science, Technology, Engineering, and Math).

Who Requires the SAT Subject Tests?

Most college websites and catalogs include information about admission requirements, including which Subject Tests are needed or recommended for admission. Schools have varying policies regarding Subject Tests, but they generally fall into one or more of the following categories:

- Required for admission

- Recommended for admission

- Required or recommended for certain majors or programs of study (e.g., engineering, honors, etc.)

- Required or recommended for certain groups of students (e.g., home-schooled students)

- Required, recommended, or accepted for course placement

- Accepted for course credit

- Accepted as an alternative to fulfill certain college admission requirements

- Accepted as an alternative to fulfill certain high school subject competencies

- Accepted and considered, especially if Subject Tests improve or enhance a student's application

In addition, the College Board provides a number of resources where you can search for information about Subject Test requirements at specific colleges.

- Visit the websites of the colleges and universities that interest you.
- Visit College Search at www.collegeboard.org.
- Purchase a copy of *The College Board College Handbook*.

Some colleges require specific tests, such as mathematics or science, so it's important to make sure you understand the policies prior to choosing which Subject Test(s) to take. If you have questions or concerns about admission policies, contact college admission officers at individual schools. They are usually pleased to meet with students interested in their schools.

Subject Tests Offered

SAT Subject Tests measure how well you know a particular subject area and your ability to apply that knowledge. SAT Subject Tests aren't connected to specific textbooks or teaching methods. The content of each test evolves to reflect the latest trends in what is taught in typical high school courses in the corresponding subject.

The tests fall into five general subject areas:

English	History	Mathematics	Science	Languages	
				Reading Only	**with Listening**
Literature	United States History	Mathematics Level 1	Biology E/M	French	Chinese
	World History	Mathematics Level 2	Chemistry	German	French
			Physics	Italian	German
				Latin	Japanese
				Modern Hebrew	Korean
				Spanish	Spanish

Who Develops the Tests

The SAT Subject Tests are part of the SAT Program of the College Board, a not-for-profit membership association of over 6,000 schools, colleges, universities, and other educational associations. Every year, the College Board serves seven million students and their parents; 24,000 high schools; and 3,800 colleges through major programs and services in college readiness, college admission, guidance, assessment, financial aid, and enrollment.

Each subject has its own test development committee, typically composed of teachers and college professors appointed for the different Subject Tests. The test questions are written and reviewed by each Subject Test Committee, under the guidance of professional test developers. The tests are rigorously developed, highly reliable assessments of knowledge and skills taught in high school classrooms.

Deciding to Take an SAT Subject Test

Which Tests Should You Take?

The SAT Subject Test(s) that you take should be based on your interests and academic strengths. The tests are a great way to indicate interest in specific majors or programs of study (e.g., engineering, pre-med, cultural studies).

You should also consider whether the colleges that you're interested in require or recommend Subject Tests. Some colleges will grant an exemption from or credit for a freshman course requirement if a student does well on a particular SAT Subject Test. Below are some things for you to consider as you decide which test(s) to take.

Think through your strengths and interests

- List the subjects in which you do well and that truly interest you.

- Think through what you might like to study in college.

- Consider whether your current admission credentials (high school grades, SAT® scores, etc.) highlight your strengths.

Consider the colleges that you're interested in

- Make a list of the colleges you're considering.

- Take some time to look into what these colleges require or what may help you stand out in the admission process.

- Use College Search to look up colleges' test requirements.

- If the colleges you're interested in require or recommend SAT Subject Tests, find out how many tests are required or recommended and in which subjects.

Take a look at your current and recent course load

- Have you completed the required course work? The best time to take SAT Subject Tests is at the end of the course, when the material is still fresh in your mind.

- Check the recommended preparation guidelines for the Subject Tests that interest you to see if you've completed the recommended course work.

- Try your hand at some SAT Subject Test practice questions on collegeboard.org or in this book.

Don't forget, regardless of admission requirements, you can enhance your college portfolio by taking Subject Tests in subject areas that you know very well.

If you're still unsure about which SAT Subject Test(s) to take, talk to your teacher or counselor about your specific situation. You can also find more information about SAT Subject Tests on collegeboard.org.

When to Take the Tests

We generally recommend that you take the Chemistry Subject Test after you complete chemistry course(s), prior to your senior year of high school, if possible. This way, you will already have your Subject Test credentials complete, allowing you to focus on your college applications in the fall of your senior year. Try to take the test soon after your courses end, when the content is still fresh in your mind. More information about the topics covered on the Chemistry Subject Test can be found later in this book.

Because not all Subject Tests are offered on every test date, be sure to check when the Subject Tests that you're interested in are offered and plan accordingly.

You should also balance this with college application deadlines. If you're interested in applying Early Decision or Early Action to any college, many colleges advise that you take the SAT Subject Tests by October or November of your senior year. For regular decision applications, some colleges will accept SAT Subject Test scores through the December administration. Use College Search to look up policies for specific colleges.

This book suggests ways you can prepare for the Subject Tests in Chemistry. Before taking a test in a subject you haven't studied recently, ask your teacher for advice about the best time to take the test. Then review the course material thoroughly over several weeks.

How to Register for the Tests

There are several ways to register for the SAT Subject Tests.

- Visit the College Board's website at www.collegeboard.org. Most students choose to register for Subject Tests on the College Board website.

- Register by telephone (for a fee) if you have registered previously for the SAT or an SAT Subject Test. Call, toll free from anywhere in the United States, 866-756-7346. From outside the United States, call 212-713-7789.

- If you do not have access to the Internet, find registration forms in *The Paper Registration Guide for the SAT and SAT Subject Tests*. You can find the booklet in a guidance office at any high school or by writing to:

> The College Board
> SAT Program
> P.O. Box 025505
> Miami, FL 33102

When you register for the SAT Subject Tests, you will have to indicate the specific Subject Tests you plan to take on the test date you select. You may take one, two, or three tests on any given test date; your testing fee will vary accordingly. Except for the Language Tests with Listening, you may change your mind on the day of the test and instead select from any of the other Subject Tests offered that day.

Student Search Service®

The Student Search Service® helps colleges find prospective students. If you take the PSAT/NMSQT, the SAT, an SAT Subject Test, or any AP Exam, you can be included in this free service.

Here's how it works: During SAT or SAT Subject Test registration, indicate that you want to be part of the Student Search. Your name is put in a database along with other information such as your address, high school grade point average, date of birth, grade level, high school, e-mail address, intended college major, and extracurricular activities.

Colleges and scholarship programs then use the Student Search to help them locate and recruit students with characteristics that might be a good match with their schools.

Here are some points to keep in mind about the Student Search Service:

- Being part of Student Search is voluntary. You may take the test even if you don't join Student Search.

- Colleges participating in the Search do not receive your exam scores. Colleges can ask for the names of students within certain score ranges, but your exact score is not reported.

- Being contacted by a college doesn't mean you have been admitted. You can be admitted only after you apply. The Student Search Service is simply a way for colleges to reach prospective students.

- Student Search Service will share your contact information only with approved colleges and scholarship programs that are recruiting students like you. Your name will never be sold to a private company or mailing list.

Keep the Tests in Perspective

Colleges that require Subject Test scores do so because the scores are useful in making admission or placement decisions. Schools that don't have specific Subject Test policies generally review them during the application process because the scores can give a fuller picture of your academic achievement. The Subject Tests are a particularly helpful tool for admission and placement programs because the tests aren't tied to specific textbooks, grading procedures, or instruction methods but are still tied to curricula. The tests provide level ground on which colleges can compare your scores with those of students who come from schools and backgrounds that may be far different from yours.

It's important to remember that test scores are just one of several factors that colleges consider in the admission process. Admission officers also look at your high school grades, letters of recommendation, extracurricular activities, essays, and other criteria. Try to keep this in mind when you are preparing for and taking Subject Tests.

Score Choice™

In March 2009, the College Board introduced Score Choice™, a feature that gives you the option to choose the scores you send to colleges by test date for the SAT and by individual test for the SAT Subject Tests — at no additional cost. Designed to reduce your test day stress, Score Choice gives you an opportunity to show colleges the scores you feel best represent your abilities. Score Choice is optional, so if you don't actively choose to use it, all of your scores will be sent automatically with your score report. Because most colleges only consider your best scores, you should still feel comfortable reporting scores from all of your tests.

REMEMBER

Score Choice gives you an opportunity to show colleges the scores you feel best represent your abilities.

More About collegeboard.org

collegeboard.org is a comprehensive tool that can help you be prepared, connected, and informed throughout the college planning and admission process. In addition to registering for the SAT and SAT Subject Tests, you can find information about other tests and services, browse the College Board Store (where you can order *The Official Study Guide for All SAT Subject Tests™* and other guides specific to Mathematics and Sciences), and send e-mails with your questions and concerns. collegeboard.org also contains free practice questions for each of the 20 SAT Subject Tests. These are an excellent supplement to this Study Guide and can help you be even more prepared on test day.

Once you create a free online account, you can print your SAT admission ticket, see your scores, and send them to schools.

More College Planning Resources The College Board offers free, comprehensive resources at Big Future™ to help you with your college planning. Visit **bigfuture.org** to put together a step-by-step plan for the entire process, from finding the right college, exploring majors and careers, and calculating costs, to applying for scholarships and financial aid.

How to Do Your Best on the SAT Subject Test

Get Ready

Give yourself plenty of time to review the material in this book before test day. The rules for the SAT Subject Tests may be different than the rules for most of the tests you've taken in high school. You're probably used to answering questions in order, spending more time answering the hard questions, and, in the hopes of getting at least partial credit, showing all your work.

When you take the SAT Subject Tests, it's OK to move around within the test section and to answer questions in any order you wish. Keep in mind that the questions go from easier to harder. You receive one point for each question answered correctly. No partial credit is given, and only those answers entered on the answer sheet are scored. For each question that you try but answer incorrectly, a fraction of a point is subtracted from the total number of correct answers. No points are added or subtracted for unanswered questions. If your final raw score includes a fraction, the score is rounded to the nearest whole number.

Avoid Surprises

Know what to expect. Become familiar with the test and test-day procedures. You'll boost your confidence and feel a lot more relaxed.

- **Know how the tests are set up.** All SAT Subject Tests are one-hour multiple-choice tests. The first page of each Subject Test includes a background questionnaire. You will be asked to fill it out before taking the test. The information is for statistical purposes only. It will not influence your test score. Your answers to the questionnaire will assist us in developing future versions of the test. You can see a sample of the background questionnaire for the Chemistry Subject Test at the start of each practice test in this book.

- **Learn the test directions.** The directions for answering the questions in this book are the same as those on the actual test. If you become familiar with the directions now, you'll leave yourself more time to answer the questions when you take the test.

- **Study the sample questions.** The more familiar you are with question formats, the more comfortable you'll feel when you see similar questions on the actual test.

- **Get to know the answer sheet.** At the back of this book, you'll find a set of sample answer sheets. The appearance of the answer sheets in this book may differ from the answer sheets you see on test day.

- **Understand how the tests are scored.** You get one point for each right answer and lose a fraction of a point for each wrong answer. You neither gain nor lose points for omitting an answer. Hard questions count the same amount as easier questions.

A Practice Test Can Help

Find out where your strengths lie and which areas you need to work on. Do a run-through of a Subject Test under conditions that are close to what they will be on test day.

- **Set aside an hour so you can take the test without interruption.** You will be given one hour to take each SAT Subject Test.

- **Prepare a desk or table that has no books or papers on it.** No books, including dictionaries, are allowed in the test room.

- **Read the instructions that precede the practice test.** On test day, you will be asked to do this before you answer the questions.

- **Remove and fill in an answer sheet from the back of this book.** You can use one answer sheet for up to three Subject Tests.

- **Use a clock or kitchen timer to time yourself.** This will help you to pace yourself and to get used to taking a test in 60 minutes.

The Day Before the Test

It's natural to be nervous. A bit of a nervous edge can keep you sharp and focused. Below are a few suggestions to help you be more relaxed as the test approaches.

Do a brief review on the day before the test. Look through the sample questions, answer explanations, and test directions in this book or on the College Board website. Keep the review brief; cramming the night before the test is unlikely to help your performance and might even make you more anxious.

REMEMBER
You are in control.
Come prepared.
Pace yourself.
Guess wisely.

The night before test day, prepare everything you need to take with you. You will need:

- your admission ticket

- an acceptable photo ID (see page 11)

- two No. 2 pencils with soft erasers. Do not bring pens or mechanical pencils.

- a watch without an audible alarm

- a snack

Know the route to the test center and any instructions for finding the entrance.

Check the time your admission ticket specifies for arrival. Arrive a little early to give yourself time to settle in.

Get a good night's sleep.

Acceptable Photo IDs

- Driver's license (with your photo)

- State-issued ID

- Valid passport

- School ID card

- Student ID form that has been prepared by your school on school stationery and includes a recognizable photo and the school seal, which overlaps the photo (go to www.collegeboard.org for more information)

The most up-to-date information about acceptable photo IDs can be found on collegeboard.org.

REMINDER   What I Need on Test Day

Make a copy of this box and post it somewhere noticeable.

I Need   **I Have**

Appropriate photo ID

Admission ticket

Two No. 2 pencils with clean soft erasers

Watch (without an audible alarm)

Snack

Bottled water

Directions to the test center

Instructions for finding the entrance on weekends

I am leaving the house at _____ a.m.

Be on time or you can't take the test.

On Test Day

You have a good reason to feel confident. You're thoroughly prepared. You're familiar with what this day will bring. You are in control.

Keep in Mind

You must be on time or you can't take the test. Leave yourself plenty of time for mishaps and emergencies.

Think positively. If you are worrying about not doing well, then your mind isn't on the test. Be as positive as possible.

Stay focused. Think only about the question in front of you. Letting your mind wander will cost you time.

Concentrate on your own test. The first thing some students do when they get stuck on a question is to look around to see how everyone else is doing. What they usually see is that others seem busy filling in their answer sheets. Instead of being concerned that you are not doing as well as everyone else, keep in mind that everyone works at a different pace. Your neighbors may not be working on the question that puzzled you. They may not even be taking the same test. Thinking about what others are doing takes you away from working on your own test.

Making an Educated Guess

Educated guesses are helpful when it comes to taking tests with multiple-choice questions; however, making random guesses is not a good idea. To correct for random guessing, a fraction of a point is subtracted for each incorrect answer. That means random guessing — guessing with no idea of an answer that might be correct — could lower your score. The best approach is to eliminate all the choices that you know are wrong. Make an educated guess from the remaining choices. If you can't eliminate any choice, move on.

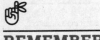

REMEMBER
All correct answers are worth one point, regardless of the question's difficulty level.

Cell phones are not allowed to be used in the test center or the testing room. If your cell phone is on, your scores will be canceled.

10 Tips FOR TAKING THE TEST

1. **Read carefully.** Consider all the choices in each question. Avoid careless mistakes that will cause you to lose points.

2. **Answer the easier questions first.** Work on less time-consuming questions before moving on to the more difficult ones.

3. **Eliminate choices that you know are wrong.** Cross them out in your test book so that you can clearly see which choices are left.

4. **Make educated guesses or skip the question.** If you have eliminated the choices that you know are wrong, guessing is your best strategy. However, if you cannot eliminate any of the answer choices, it is best to skip the question.

5. **Keep your answer sheet neat.** The answer sheet is scored by a machine, which can't tell the difference between an answer and a doodle. If the machine mistakenly reads two answers for one question, it will consider the question unanswered.

6. **Use your test booklet as scrap paper.** Use it to make notes or write down ideas. No one else will look at what you write.

7. **Check off questions as you work on them.** This will save time and help you to know which questions you've skipped.

8. **Check your answer sheet regularly.** Make sure you are in the right place. Check the number of the question and the number on the answer sheet every few questions. This is especially important when you skip a question. Losing your place on the answer sheet will cost you time and may cost you points.

9. **Work at an even, steady pace and keep moving.** Each question on the test takes a certain amount of time to read and answer. Good test-takers develop a sense of timing to help them complete the test. Your goal is to spend time on the questions that you are most likely to answer correctly.

10. **Keep track of time.** During the hour that each Subject Test takes, check your progress occasionally so that you know how much of the test you have completed and how much time is left. Leave a few minutes for review toward the end of the testing period.

IMPORTANT

If you erase all your answers to a Subject Test, that's the same as a request to cancel the test. All Subject Tests taken with the erased test will also be canceled.

7 Ways
TO PACE YOURSELF

1. Set up a schedule. Know when you should be one-quarter of the way through and halfway through. Every now and then, check your progress against your schedule.

2. Begin to work as soon as the testing time begins. Reading the instructions and getting to know the test directions in this book ahead of time will allow you to do that.

3. Work at an even, steady pace. After you answer the questions you are sure of, move on to those for which you'll need more time.

4. Skip questions you can't answer. You might have time to return to them. Remember to mark them in your test booklet, so you'll be able to find them later.

5. As you work on a question, cross out the answers you can eliminate in your test book.

6. Go back to the questions you skipped. If you can, eliminate some of the answer choices, then make an educated guess.

7. Leave time in the last few minutes to check your answers to avoid mistakes.

After the Tests

Most, but not all, scores will be reported online several weeks after the test date. A few days later, a full score report will be available to you online. Your score report will also be mailed to your high school and to the colleges, universities, and scholarship programs that you indicated on your registration form or on the correction form attached to your admission ticket. The score report includes your scores, percentiles, and interpretive information. You will only receive a paper score report if you indicate that you would like one.

What's Your Score?

Scores are available for free at www.collegeboard.org several weeks after each SAT is given. You can also get your scores — for a fee — by telephone. Call Customer Service at (866) 756-7346 in the United States. From outside the United States, dial (212) 713-7789.

Some scores may take longer to report. If your score report is not available online when expected, check back the following week. If you have not received your mailed score report by eight weeks after the test date (by five weeks for online reports), contact Customer Service by phone at (866) 756-7346 or by e-mail at sat@info.collegeboard.org.

Should You Take the Tests Again?

Before you decide whether or not to retest, you need to evaluate your scores. The best way to evaluate how you really did on a Subject Test is to compare your scores to the admissions or placement requirements, or average scores, of the colleges to which you are applying. You may decide that with additional work you could do better taking the test again.

? Contacting the College Board

If you have comments or questions about the tests, please write to us at the College Board SAT Program, P.O. Box 025505, Miami, FL 33102, or e-mail us at sat@info.collegeboard.org.

Chemistry

Purpose

The Subject Test in Chemistry measures the understanding of chemistry you would be expected to have after successfully completing a college preparatory course in high school and is designed to be independent of the particular textbook or instructional approach used.

Format

This is a one-hour test with 85 multiple-choice questions.

Content

The test covers the topics listed in the chart on the next page. Different aspects of these topics are stressed from year to year. However, because high school courses differ, both in the amount of time devoted to each major topic and in the specific subtopics covered, it is likely that most students will encounter some questions on topics with which they are not familiar. Every edition of the test contains approximately five questions on equation balancing and/or predicting products of chemical reactions; these are distributed among the various content categories.

Topics Covered

Topics	Approximate Percentage of Test
I. Structure of Matter	25%

Atomic Structure, including experimental evidence of atomic structure, quantum numbers and energy levels (orbitals), electron configurations, periodic trends

Molecular Structure, including Lewis structures, three-dimensional molecular shapes, polarity

Bonding, including ionic, covalent, and metallic bonds; relationships of bonding to properties and structures; intermolecular forces such as hydrogen bonding, dipole-dipole forces, dispersion (London) forces

II. States of Matter	16%

Gases, including the kinetic molecular theory, gas law relationships, molar volumes, density, stoichiometry

Liquids and Solids, including intermolecular forces in liquids and solids, types of solids, phase changes, and phase diagrams

Solutions, including molarity and percent by mass concentrations; solution preparation and stoichiometry; factors affecting solubility of solids, liquids, and gases; qualitative aspects of colligative properties

III. Reaction Types	14%

Acids and Bases, including Brønsted-Lowry theory, strong and weak acids and bases, pH, titrations, indicators

Oxidation-Reduction, including recognition of oxidation-reduction reactions, combustion, oxidation numbers, use of activity series

Precipitation, including basic solubility rules

IV. Stoichiometry	14%

Mole Concept, including molar mass, Avogadro's number, empirical and molecular formulas

Chemical Equations, including the balancing of equations, stoichiometric calculations, percent yield, limiting reactants

V. Equilibrium and Reaction Rates	5%

Equilibrium Systems, including factors affecting position of equilibrium (LeChâtelier's principle) in gaseous and aqueous systems, equilibrium constants, equilibrium expressions

Rates of Reactions, including factors affecting reaction rates, potential energy diagrams, activation energies

VI. Thermochemistry	6%

Including conservation of energy, calorimetry and specific heats, enthalpy (heat) changes associated with phase changes and chemical reactions, heating and cooling curves, randomness (entropy)

VII. Descriptive Chemistry	12%

Including common elements, nonmenclature of ions and compounds, periodic trends in chemical and physical properties of the elements, reactivity of elements and prediction of products of chemical reactions, examples of simple organic compounds and compounds of environmental concern

VIII. Laboratory	8%

Including knowledge of laboratory equipment, measurements, procedures, observations, safety, calculations, data analysis, interpretation of graphical data, drawing conclusions from observations and data

Skills Specifications	Approximate Percentage of Test
Recall of Knowledge	**20%**
Remembering fundamental concepts and specific information; demonstrating familiarity with terminology	
Application of Knowledge	**45%**
Applying a single principle to unfamiliar and/or practical situations to obtain a qualitative result or solve a quantitative problem	
Synthesis of Knowledge	**35%**
Inferring and deducing from qualitative data and/or quantitative data; integrating two or more relationships to draw conclusions or solve problems	

How to Prepare

- Take a one-year introductory chemistry course at the college preparatory level.

- Laboratory experience is a significant factor in developing reasoning and problem-solving skills and should help in test preparation even though laboratory skills can be tested only in a limited way in a multiple-choice test.

- Mathematics preparation that enables handling simple algebraic relationships and applying these to solving word problems will help.

- Familiarize yourself with the concepts of ratio and direct and inverse proportions, exponents, and scientific notation.

- Familiarize yourself with directions in advance. The directions in this book are identical to those that appear on the test.

You should have the ability to

- recall and understand the major concepts of chemistry and to apply the principles to solve specific problems in chemistry.

- organize and interpret results obtained by observation and experimentation and to draw conclusions or make inferences from experimental data, including data presented in graphic and/or tabular form.

Notes: (1) A periodic table indicating the atomic numbers and masses of elements is provided for all test administrations.

    (2) Calculators aren't allowed to be used during the test.

    (3) Problem solving requires simple numerical calculations.

    (4) The metric system of units is used.

Score

The total score is reported on the 200 to 800 scale.

Sample Questions

Three types of questions are used in the Chemistry Subject Test: classification questions, relationship analysis questions, and five-choice completion questions.

Note: For all questions involving solutions, assume that the solvent is water unless otherwise noted.

Classification Questions

Each set of classification questions has, in the heading, five lettered choices that you will use to answer all of the questions in the set. The choices may be statements that refer to concepts, principles, substances, or observable phenomena or they may be graphs, pictures, equations, numbers, or experimental settings or situations.

Because the same five choices are applicable to several questions, the classification questions usually require less reading than other types of multiple-choice questions. Answering a question correctly depends on the sophistication of the set of questions. One set may test your ability to recall information; another set may ask you to apply information to a specific situation or to translate information from one form to another (descriptive, graphical, mathematical). The directions for this type of question specifically state that you should not eliminate a choice simply because it is the correct answer to a previous question.

Following are the directions for and an example of a classification set.

Directions: Each set of lettered choices below refers to the numbered statements immediately following it. Select the one lettered choice that best fits each statement or answers each question and then fill in the corresponding circle on the answer sheet. A choice may be used once, more than once, or not at all in each set.

Note: For all questions involving solutions, assume that the solvent is water unless otherwise stated.

Throughout the test, the following symbols have the definitions specified unless otherwise noted.

H	=	enthalpy	atm	=	atmosphere(s)
M	=	molar	g	=	gram(s)
n	=	number of moles	J	=	joule(s)
P	=	pressure	kJ	=	kilojoule(s)
R	=	molar gas constant	L	=	liter(s)
S	=	entropy	mL	=	milliliter(s)
T	=	temperature	mm	=	millimeter(s)
V	=	volume	mol	=	mole(s)
			V	=	volt(s)

Questions 1–3 refer to the following topics and relationships concerning states of matter.

A) A general rule for predicting solubility

B) Solid phase changing to the liquid phase

C) A state in which the liquid and gas phases are in equilibrium

D) Relationship between volume and temperature at constant pressure

E) Relationship between absolute temperature and the kinetic energy of particles

1

Particles in a substance vibrate faster and faster until some are able to break from their fixed positions and move around more freely.

Choice (B) is the correct answer. In a solid, particles are fixed in position in a lattice structure but are not motionless. When heated, particles in a solid gain energy and freedom of motion as the solid melts and becomes a liquid. Although particles in a liquid have freedom of motion, they are still close together.

2

Evaporation and condensation rates in a closed container are the same.

Choice (C) is the correct answer. When the liquid and gas phases are in equilibrium in a closed container, the number of particles leaving the liquid (evaporation) is equal to the number of particles entering the liquid from the gas phase (condensation).

3

The spaces between gas particles in air increase as the temperature of the air increases.

Choice (D) is the correct answer. Charles's Law describes the direct relationship of temperature and volume of a gas. Assuming that pressure does not change, a doubling in absolute temperature of a gas causes a doubling of the volume of that gas. A decrease in absolute temperature is proportional to the decrease in volume.

Questions 4–6 refer to the following information.

$$H_2SO_4(aq) + Zn(s) \rightarrow H_2(g) + ZnSO_4(aq)$$
$$AgNO_3(aq) + KI(aq) \rightarrow KNO_3(aq) + AgI(s)$$
$$HF(aq) + H_2O(l) \leftrightharpoons F^-(aq) + H_3O^+(aq)$$

A) $Zn(s)$

B) $H_2(g)$

C) $AgI(s)$

D) $H_2O(l)$

E) $H_3O^+(aq)$

4

Which species is classified as an insoluble salt?

Choice (C) is the correct answer. As a solid, this species is formed in the reaction as a precipitate, or insoluble solid. Also, AgI is the only listed species that is a salt, or a neutral compound made of positive and negative ions. The second reaction is a precipitation reaction, showing two salts are switching ion pairs from $Ag^+NO_3^-$ and K^+I^- to $K^+NO_3^-$ and the insoluble salt Ag^+I^-.

5

Which species is the acid of a conjugate acid–base pair?

Choice (E) is the correct answer. The Brønsted-Lowry acid base theory says that an acid donates a proton to a base, which accepts the proton. After the acid reactant donates a proton to the base reactant, the acid reactant becomes the conjugate base product, and the base reactant becomes the conjugate acid product. The HF is the acid that donates a proton to become the conjugate base, F^-. H_2O is the base that accepts the proton to become the conjugate acid, H_3O^+. The third reaction is the only acid–base reaction. Although the first reaction involves a strong acid, it is not an acid–base reaction because there is no proton transfer between the reactants.

6

Which species is acting as a reducing agent?

Choice (A) is the correct answer. The first reaction is the only reduction–oxidation reaction, and the reducing agent loses electrons and increases its oxidation state, or hypothetical charge. In this case, Zn loses two electrons and is oxidized to Zn^{2+}. In the process, it is the agent that reduces H^+ to elemental $H°$.

Questions 7–9 refer to the following elements.

A) Al, aluminum

B) C, carbon

C) Ca, calcium

D) F, fluorine

E) Li, lithium

7

Which element is the most electronegative of all elements?

Choice (D) is the correct answer. As you move from left to right across a row in the periodic table, electronegativity increases due to the stronger attraction that atoms obtain as the nuclear charge increases. As you move down a group in the periodic table, electronegativity decreases because the atomic number increases, increasing the distance between the valence electrons and nucleus. The exceptions are the noble or inert gases, because they already have a complete valence shell, and the lanthanides and actinides that do not follow these trends. Fluorine's position at the top right corner of the periodic table corresponds with the fact that it is the most electronegative element.

8

Which element reacts with oxygen in a 2 to 3 ratio of element to oxygen, producing X_2O_3?

Choice (A) is the correct answer. Aluminum has an oxidation state of +3 in the majority of Al-containing compounds, and oxygen commonly has an oxidation state of −2. In order for a molecule with 3 oxygen atoms to have a neutral charge, something must balance out the $(3)(-2) = -6$ charge. Here, the 2 Al ions contribute a charge of $(2)(+3) = 6$ to give a neutral compound. The other elements do not have the oxidation states for making a neutral compound if 2 atoms were to react with 3 oxygen atoms.

9

Which element often forms compounds in which it has four covalent bonds?

Choice (B) is the correct answer. Carbon has four valence electrons and often forms four single bonds with other nonmetals. Students should recognize that this is the basis of organic chemistry.

Relationship Analysis Questions

This type of question consists of a specific statement or assertion (Statement I) followed by an explanation of the assertion (Statement II). The question is answered by determining if the assertion and the explanation are each true statements and, if so, whether the explanation (or reason) provided does, in fact, properly explain the statement given in the assertion.

This type of question tests your ability to identify proper cause-and-effect relationships. It probes whether you can assess the correctness of the original assertion and then evaluate the truth of the "reason" proposed to justify it. The analysis required by this type of question provides you with an opportunity to demonstrate developed reasoning skills and the scope of your understanding of a particular topic.

> On the actual Chemistry Test, the following type of question must be answered on a special section (labeled "Chemistry") at the lower left-hand corner of your answer sheet. These questions will be numbered beginning with 101 and must be answered according to the following directions.
>
> **SAMPLE ANSWER GRID**

Directions: Each question below consists of two statements: I in the left-hand column and II in the right-hand column. For each question, determine whether statement I is true or false <u>and</u> whether statement II is true or false and fill in the corresponding T or F circles on your answer sheet. <u>Fill in circle CE only if statement II is a correct explanation of the true statement I.</u>

EXAMPLES:

I		II
EX 1. H_2SO_4 is a strong acid	BECAUSE	H_2SO_4 contains sulfur.
EX 2. An atom of oxygen is electrically neutral	BECAUSE	an oxygen atom contains an equal number of protons and electrons.

SAMPLE ANSWERS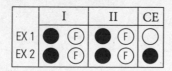

I		II

10

| Sodium and chlorine have different chemical properties | BECAUSE | sodium and chlorine have different principal quantum numbers for the highest occupied energy level. |

I True, II False, not CE is the correct answer. Sodium (Na) and chlorine (Cl) have different chemical properties because they have different numbers of valence electrons. Elements in different groups of the periodic table have vastly different chemical properties because they have different numbers of valence electrons in their outer shells. Sodium and chlorine have the *same* principal quantum number for the highest energy electron because they are in the same period; this is true for any of the elements in the first three rows of the periodic table.

11

| When 1.0 mol H_2SO_4 reacts with 1.0 mol NaOH according to the reaction by the equation above, NaOH is the limiting reactant | BECAUSE | in the reaction represented by the equation above, the molar mass of H_2SO_4 is more than twice the molar mass of NaOH. |

I True, II True, CE No is the correct answer. The stoichiometry shows that 1.0 mol of NaOH will react with only 0.5 mol of H_2SO_4, leaving 0.5 mol of H_2SO_4 unreacted, indicating that NaOH is the limiting reactant. The molar mass of H_2SO_4 is 98.08 g/mol, which is more than twice NaOH's molar mass of 40.00 g/mol. However, the molar masses are not relevant because the limiting reactant is determined by mole ratios, not by the molar masses of the reactants.

<u>I</u>   <u>II</u>

$2 NO_2(g) \leftrightarrows N_2O_4(g)$

12

When the reaction represented by the equation above is at equilibrium in a sealed container, a decrease in the volume of the reaction container will shift the equilibrium toward NO_2 BECAUSE   in the reaction represented above, a shift toward NO_2 decreases the pressure of the system.

I False, II False, CE No is the correct answer. PV is constant; as volume decreases, the pressure will increase. To accommodate for this volume change, the equilibrium will shift in the direction that decreases the number of moles of gas. Because the formation of N_2O_4 uses 2 moles and produces only 1, the number of moles will decrease, countering the increased pressure. Therefore, increasing pressure will produce more N_2O_4, shifting the equilibrium to the right.

13

Evaporation of water results in an increase in entropy   BECAUSE   water molecules are distributed more randomly in the gas state than in the liquid state.

I True, II True, CE Yes is the correct answer. Entropy is a measure of disorder in a system. Ice is more ordered than liquid water, which is more ordered than the particles in water vapor. Intermolecular forces in the liquid state result in an ordered, but fluid, arrangement of molecules, but these forces are not a factor in the gas state because the intermolecular distances are much greater. The fact that molecules of water in the gas state have a higher entropy than liquid water molecules corresponds with an increase in entropy during evaporation.

I   II

14

| When magnesium (Mg) reacts with chlorine (Cl), the atoms combine in a 1 to 2 ratio to form $MgCl_2$ | BECAUSE | each magnesium atom gains two electrons and each chlorine atom loses one electron. |

I True, II False, CE No is the correct answer. Magnesium (Mg) is divalent and chlorine (Cl) is monovalent. The 1 to 2 ratio gives each atom a complete octet of electrons. Therefore, one atom of Mg would react with two atoms of Cl to produce $MgCl_2$. Alkaline earth metals in group 2 have two valence electrons and they tend to react to lose those electrons. Halogens are one electron short of an octet, so they tend to react to gain one electron. When $MgCl_2$ is formed, each magnesium atom would lose two electrons, and each chlorine atom would gain one electron.

15

| If the volume on a buret can be accurately read to the nearest 0.01 mL, then the volume of exactly 20 mL of a solution released from the buret should be recorded as 20.00 mL | BECAUSE | it is standard practice to record data to two decimal places. |

I True, II False, CE No is the correct answer. Because the buret can be read accurately to 0.01 mL, the volume of a solution should be measured using two decimal places. However, the standard practice is to record data and report measurements using correct significant figures, not just to use two decimal places. Statement II is not the correct explanation of statement I, because the standard practice is stated incorrectly.

Five-Choice Completion Questions

The five-choice completion question is written either as an incomplete statement or as a question. It is appropriate when (1) the problem presented is clearly delineated by the wording of the question so that you are asked to choose not a universal solution but the best of the solutions offered; (2) the problem is such that you are required to evaluate the relevance of five plausible, or even scientifically accurate, options and to select the one most pertinent; (3) the problem has several pertinent solutions and you are required to select the one inappropriate solution that is presented. Such questions normally contain a word in capital letters such as NOT, LEAST, or EXCEPT.

A special type of five-choice completion question is used in some tests, including the SAT Subject Test in Chemistry, to allow for the possibility of multiple correct answers. For these questions, you must evaluate each response independently of the others in order to select the most appropriate combination. In questions of this type, several (usually three or four) statements labeled by Roman numerals are given with the question. One or more of these statements may correctly answer the question. You must select, from among the five lettered choices that follow, the one combination of statements that best answers the question. In the test, questions of this type are intermixed among the more standard five-choice completion questions. (Question 8 is an example of this type of question.)

In five-choice completion questions, you may be asked to convert the information given in a word problem into graphical form or to select and apply the mathematical relationship necessary to solve the scientific problem. Alternatively, you may be asked to interpret experimental data, graphical stimuli, or mathematical expressions.

When the experimental data or other scientific problems to be analyzed are comparatively extensive, it is often convenient to organize several five-choice completion questions into sets, that is, direct each question in a set to the same material. This practice allows you to answer several questions based on the same material. In no case, however, is the answer to one question necessary for answering a subsequent question correctly. Each question in a set is independent of the others and refers only to the material given for the entire set.

Directions: Each of the questions or incomplete statements below is followed by five suggested answers or completions. Select the one that is best in each case and then fill in the corresponding circle on the answer sheet.

16

$$H \! : \! \ddot{N} \! : \! H$$
$$H$$

This is the Lewis structure of an ammonia (NH_3) molecule.

Based on the Lewis electron-dot diagram shown above, which of the following best describes the shape of an ammonia molecule?

A) T-shaped

B) Tetrahedral

C) Square planar

D) Trigonal planar

E) Trigonal pyramidal

Choice (E) is the correct answer. The lone pair on the N atom repels the bonding electrons of the three NH bonds to create a three-legged stool shape. According to valence shell electron pair repulsion (VSEPR) theory, the shape of the molecule and the angles between bonds are determined by the repulsion of all valence shell electrons. The lone electron pair and the three NH bonding electron pairs repel each other toward the apexes of a tetrahedron. Because the lone pair is not part of the molecular shape, the result is that the three bonds form a three-sided pyramid and are separated by an angle slightly less than the tetrahedral angle, 109.5°.

17

The air trapped in a glass tube occupies 2.0 liters at 1.0 atm. The sample of air is compressed until the pressure on the trapped air molecules is increased to 4.0 atm. Assuming constant temperature, what is the new volume of the air (in L)?

A) 0.25L

B) 0.50L

C) 2.0L

D) 4.0L

E) 8.0L

Choice (B) is the correct answer. The ideal gas law can be used to determine new values for a gas based on changing conditions. Rearranging the ideal gas law formula, $PV = nRT$, and solving for the universal gas constant, R, results in $R = PV/nT$. When comparing a gas at two different conditions, you can set the two conditions equal to each other: $P_1V_1/n_1T_1 = P_2V_2/n_2T_2$. Because temperature ($T$) and amount of gas ($n$) are constant in this situation, the equation simplifies to $P_1V_1 = P_2V_2$. Solving for the final volume results in $V_2 = P_1V_1/P_2$. Plugging in the initial volume and pressure and final pressure for the gas gives $V_2 = (1.0atm)(2.0L)/(4.0L) = 0.50L$.

18

Which of these properties generally decreases when moving left to right across a period, or row, of the periodic table?

A) Reactivity

B) Atomic radius

C) Electron affinity

D) First ionization energy

E) Number of valence electrons

Choice (B) is the correct answer. Atomic radii decrease from left to right because the effective nuclear charge of atoms increases across the rows, drawing the valence shell electrons closer. Choice (A) is incorrect because reactivity first decreases as the tendency to lose electrons decreases, then increases as the tendency to gain electrons increases. Choices (C) and (D) are both incorrect because electrons become more tightly held as the number of protons and electrons increase, resulting in increasing electron affinity and ionization energy. Choice (E) is incorrect because each element has one more valence electron than the previous element.

19

Which of these represents the ground-state electron configuration of a neutral aluminum (Al) atom?

A) $1s^2 2s^2 2p^1$

B) $1s^2 2s^2 2p^6 3s^1$

C) $1s^2 2s^2 2p^6 3s^2 3p^1$

D) $1s^2 2s^2 2p^6 3s^2 3p^5$

E) $1s^2 2s^2 2p^6 3s^2 3p^6 3d^1 4s^2$

Choice (C) is the correct answer. Aluminum has the configuration of neon ($1s^2 2s^2 2p^6$) plus a full 3s orbital and one electron in the 3p orbital. Choice (A) is the configuration of boron (just above aluminum), choice (B) is the configuration of sodium, choice (D) is the configuration of chlorine and choice (E) is the configuration of scandium.

20

Which of the following molecules is nonpolar but has polar bonds?

A) Carbon dioxide (CO_2)

B) Hydrogen chloride (HCl)

C) Water (H_2O)

D) Sulfur dioxide (SO_2)

E) Phosphorus trichloride (PCl_3)

Choice (A) is the correct answer. The electronegativity difference between carbon and oxygen is large enough to make these bonds polar, but the overall molecule is nonpolar because it is linear. Choices (B), (C), (D), and (E) are polar molecules with polar bonds. Choices (C), (D), and (E) are polar because of geometry.

21

Substance	Molar mass (g)	Boiling point (°C)
Methane	16	-162
Water	18	100

The table above lists the molar masses and boiling points of methane and water at standard pressure. Which of the following best explains the large difference between the boiling points of methane and water?

A) Methane is an organic compound.

B) Water needs more energy to boil because it ionizes into hydrogen and hydroxide ions.

C) Most compounds that contain oxygen have high boiling points

D) London dispersion forces are not present for simple hydrocarbons with low molar mass.

E) Hydrogen bonding in water increases the attractive forces between molecules.

Choice (E) is the correct answer. The value of a boiling point reflects the strengths of the intermolecular forces between liquid molecules. In order to boil, liquid molecules must overcome these attractive forces to separate and form a vapor. Water molecules have very strong, attractive forces because they form hydrogen bonds. Water molecules are also polar, with large dipoles that attract each other. Methane cannot form hydrogen bonds, and it is nonpolar. The only attractive forces between methane molecules are London dispersion forces. Choice (A) is incorrect because many organic compounds have higher boiling points than water. Choice (B) is incorrect because ionization is different from boiling. Ionization requires the covalent bonds between molecules to break; this requires a lot more energy than boiling, which is the liquid molecules overcoming attractive forces so they can form vapors. Choice (C) is not correct because there is not a connection between whether or not a compound contains oxygen and its boiling point. Choice (D) is incorrect because London dispersion forces are the most important intermolecular force for hydrocarbons.

22

Which of the following best explains how some nonpolar substances can be liquids at room temperature?

A) The molecules share electrons, forming bonds.

B) The molecules form temporary dipoles with partial charges.

C) The molecules transfer electrons, forming ions with opposite charges.

D) The molecules form positive ions that are held together by free electrons.

E) The molecules form temporary bonds between hydrogen and electronegative atoms.

Choice (B) is the correct answer. In liquids, the intermolecular attractive forces are strong enough to hold molecules close together. Because of the nature of the electron cloud, there are temporary dipoles in nonpolar molecules that can induce dipoles in nearby molecules. The induced dipoles cause the molecules to attract each other. Choices (A), (C), and (D) are incorrect because they describe covalent, ionic, and metallic bonding, respectively. Choice (E) is incorrect because it describes hydrogen bonding, which is not a feature of nonpolar substances.

23

The phase diagram for carbon dioxide (CO_2) is shown to the right. Crossing through which of the following represents a phase change directly from solid to gas?

A) point Y

B) point Z

C) line WX

D) line XY

E) line XZ

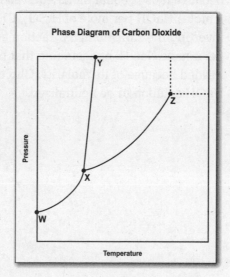

Choice (C) is the correct answer. Crossing segment WX (by decreasing pressure, increasing temperature, or both) represents a phase change directly from solid to gas, otherwise known as sublimation. Above the segment, carbon dioxide is solid, and below the segment, it is gas. At the segment, the two phases of matter are in equilibrium. Choice (A) is an arbitrary point between solid and liquid phases. Choice (B) represents the point past which there is no physical distinction between vapor and liquid phases. Choice (D) represents a change between solid and liquid, and choice (E) represents a change between liquid and gas.

24

How many milliliters of 0.20 M sulfuric acid (H_2SO_4) solution will be needed to exactly neutralize 200 mL of 0.10 M sodium hydroxide (NaOH) solution?

A) 50.0 mL

B) 80.0 mL

C) 100 mL

D) 200 mL

E) 400 mL

Choice (A) is the correct answer. Sodium hydroxide = NaOH = 1 mol Na^+ and 1 mol OH^-. Sulfuric acid = H_2SO_4 = 2 mol H^+ and 1 mol SO_4^{2-}. Therefore, to neutralize 1 mol of sulfuric acid (2 mol H^+), you need 2 mol of sodium hydroxide (2 × 1 mol OH^-).

(200 mL) × (1 L / 1000 mL) = 0.2 L
0.10 M = 0.1 mol/ 1 L
0.20 M = 0.2 mol/ 1 L

Therefore: (0.20 L NaOH) × (0.10 mol NaOH/L) ×
(1 mol H_2SO_4/2 mol NaOH) × (1L/0.20 mol H_2SO_4) = 0.050 L = 50 mL

Choice (B) is the mass of two moles of NaOH. Choice (C) is incorrect because it uses equal molar equivalents of NaOH and H_2SO_4 rather than 2 moles NaOH per mole of H_2SO_4. Choice (D) could be the result of inverting the stoichiometry fraction and calculating for 2 moles H_2SO_4 per 1 mole NaOH, or assuming that half as much H_2SO_4 solution is needed because of its molarity. Choice (E) is two times the amount of NaOH solution to be neutralized.

25

Solution	Concentration (mol/L)	pH
I	0.1	14
II	0.1	2.9
III	0.01	2.0
IV	0.001	3.0

The table shown above describes four solutions needed for an acid–base laboratory experiment. Which solution(s) were prepared using weak acids?

A) I only

B) II only

C) I and II only

D) III and IV only

E) II, III, and IV

Choice (B) is the correct answer. The data for Solution II are based on a dilute acetic acid solution. Together, the concentration of 0.1 M and pH of 2.9 indicate that the solution most likely contains a weak acid. These data demonstrate that the acid does not completely dissociate (else the pH would be 1.0). Solution I is a strong base in choices (A) and (C). Solutions III and IV, in choices (D) and (E), are both examples of strong acids. For all three of these solutions, the concentrations and pH values together demonstrate that they completely dissociate.

26

$$2\ KMnO_4 + 3\ Na_2SO_3 + H_2O \rightarrow 2\ MnO_2 + 3\ Na_2SO_4 + 2\ KOH$$

Potassium permanganate ($KMnO_4$) reacts with sodium sulfite (Na_2SO_3) in water to produce manganese dioxide (MnO_2), sodium sulfate (Na_2SO_4), and potassium hydroxide (KOH), as shown by the equation above

A) K^+

B) MnO_4^-

C) Na^+

D) SO_3^{2-}

E) H_2O

Choice (D) is the correct answer. SO_3^{2-} is the reducing agent, or reductant, in this reaction because it is oxidized to SO_4^{2-}. The oxidation state of sulfur in SO_3^{2-} is +4: $(+4 \times 1) + (-2 \times 3) = -2$. The oxidation state of sulfur in SO_4^{2-} is +6 to give the sulfate ion a −2 charge: $(+6 \times 1) + (-2 \times 4) = -2$. Choice (B) is wrong because MnO_4^- is reduced to MnO_2; the oxidation state of Mn decreases from +7 to +4, so MnO_4^- is an oxidizing agent. Choices (A), (C), and (E) are incorrect because the elements K, Na, H, and O do not change oxidation state.

27

Analysis of a sample of an unknown hydrocarbon yields 2.4 g of carbon and 0.30 g of hydrogen. These results indicate an empirical formula of C_2H_3. Based on this information and the usual bonding patterns of the atoms involved, which of these formulas COULD be the molecular formula?

A) C_2H_6

B) C_3H_4

C) C_3H_6

D) C_4H_6

E) C_6H_9

Choice (D) is the correct answer. Empirical formulas state the simplest ratio of atoms for each element in a compound. Choice (D) is correct because C_4H_6 is the simplest molecular formula for the given empirical formula. C_4H_6 can be the formula for both butadiene (a linear 4-carbon chain with 2 double bonds) and cyclobutene (a 4-carbon chain cycloalkene). Choices (A), (B), and (C) are incorrect because the C:H ratio must be 2:3. Choice (E) is not possible; a 6-carbon hydrocarbon will only have an even number of hydrogen atoms.

28

An analytical chemist is given a sample of aluminum oxide (Al_2O_3). She finds that it contains approximately 12 moles of oxygen. Knowing that the atomic mass of aluminum is 27 g/mol and the atomic mass of oxygen is 16 g/mol, what is the total mass of this Al_2O_3 sample?

A)   102 g

B)   192 g

C)   408 g

D) 1,224 g

E) 3,672 g

Choice (C) is the correct answer. Using the atomic mass of aluminum and oxygen, calculate the molar mass of Al_2O_3:

2 mol Al × (27 g/ mol) = 54 g/mol

3 mol O × (16 g/mol) = 48 g/mol

Al_2O_3 = 54 g/mol + 48 g/mol = 102 g/mol

Next, knowing the moles of oxygen in the Al_2O_3 sample (12), that there are 3 moles of oxygen in every mole Al_2O_3, and the atomic mass of Al_2O_3, calculate the mass of the sample:

12 mol O × (1 mol Al_2O_3/3 mol O) × (102 g Al_2O_3/1 mol Al_2O_3) = 408 g Al_2O_3.

Choice (A) is the mass of 1 mol of aluminum (III) oxide. Choice (B) is the mass of 12 mols of oxygen. Choice (D) ignores the stoichiometry fraction, and choice (E) inverts the stoichiometry fraction.

29

$$\ldots C_3H_8O + \ldots O_2 \rightarrow \ldots CO_2 + \ldots H_2O$$

The equation above represents the complete combustion of propanol (C_3H_8O). When this equation is balanced and all coefficients are reduced to lowest whole number terms, the coefficient for O_2 is

A) 6

B) 8

C) 9

D) 12

E) 18

Choice (C) is the correct answer. The balanced equation is $2\ C_3H_8O + 9\ O_2 \rightarrow 6\ CO_2 + 8\ H_2O$. The coefficient for O_2 is 9. Choices (A) and (B) are the coefficients of the products. Choice (D) is the sum of the coefficients of the products minus the coefficient of C_3H_8O. Choice (E) is the number of oxygen *atoms* in the balanced chemical equation (ignoring the subscript, 2, in the O_2 molecule).

30

The graph to the right shows how potential energy changes during a chemical reaction. Which aspect of the graph provides the best evidence that the chemical reaction is exothermic?

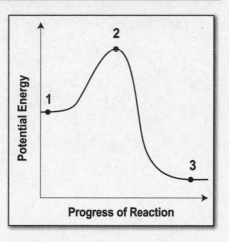

A) The potential energy at point 2

B) The time needed to reach point 3

C) The time elapsed between points 2 and 3

D) The energy difference between points 1 and 2

E) The energy difference between points 1 and 3

Choice (E) is the correct answer. This is the potential energy difference between reactants and products. Because the change is negative, the reaction must release energy, so it is exothermic. Choice (A) is the potential energy of the transition state, when the reaction always has the highest potential energy. Choices (B) and (C) may provide information about the reaction rate but not about whether the reaction is exothermic. Choice (D) is the activation energy, which is the amount of energy the reaction needs to proceed.

Chemistry Subject Test - Practice Test 1

Practice Helps

The test that follows is an actual, previously administered SAT Subject Test in Chemistry. To get an idea of what it's like to take this test, practice under conditions that are much like those of an actual test administration.

- Set aside an hour when you can take the test uninterrupted.

- Sit at a desk or table with no other books or papers. Dictionaries, other books, or notes are not allowed in the test room.

- Tear out an answer sheet from the back of this book and fill it in just as you would on the day of the test. One answer sheet can be used for up to three Subject Tests.

- Read the instructions that precede the practice test. During the actual administration you will be asked to read them before answering test questions.

- Time yourself by placing a clock or kitchen timer in front of you.

- After you finish the practice test, read the sections "How to Score the SAT Subject Test in Chemistry" and "How Did You Do on the Subject Test in Chemistry?"

- The appearance of the answer sheet in this book may differ from the answer sheet you see on test day.

CHEMISTRY TEST

The top portion of the page of the answer sheet that you will use to take the Chemistry Test must be filled in exactly as illustrated below. When your supervisor tells you to fill in the circle next to the name of the test you are about to take, mark your answer sheet as shown.

After filling in the circle next to the name of the test you are taking, locate the Background Questions section, which also appears at the top of your answer sheet (as shown above). This is where you will answer the following Background Questions on your answer sheet.

BACKGROUND QUESTIONS

Please answer the four questions below by filling in the appropriate circle in the Background Questions box on your answer sheet. <u>The information you provide is for statistical purposes only and will not affect your test score.</u>

Question I

How many semesters of chemistry have you taken in high school? (If you are taking chemistry this semester, count it as a full semester.) Fill in only <u>one</u> circle of circles 1-3.

- One semester or less   —Fill in circle 1.
- Two semesters   —Fill in circle 2.
- Three semesters or more   —Fill in circle 3.

Question II

How recently have you studied chemistry?

- I am currently enrolled in or have
  just completed a chemistry course.   —Fill in circle 4.
- I have not studied chemistry for
  6 months or more.   —Fill in circle 5.

Question III

Which of the following best describes your preparation in algebra? (If you are taking an algebra course this semester, count it as a full semester.) Fill in only <u>one</u> circle of circles 6-8.

- One semester or less   —Fill in circle 6.
- Two semesters   —Fill in circle 7.
- Three semesters or more   —Fill in circle 8.

Question IV

Are you currently taking Advanced Placement Chemistry? If you are, fill in circle 9.

When the supervisor gives the signal, turn the page and begin the Chemistry Test. There is a total of 85 questions in the Chemistry Test (1-70 plus questions 101-115 that must be answered on the special section at the lower left-hand corner of the answer sheet).

CHEMISTRY TEST

MATERIAL IN THE FOLLOWING TABLE MAY BE USEFUL IN ANSWERING THE QUESTIONS IN THIS EXAMINATION.

PERIODIC TABLE OF THE ELEMENTS

DO NOT DETACH FROM BOOK.

1 H 1.0079																		2 He 4.0026
3 Li 6.941	4 Be 9.012											5 B 10.811	6 C 12.011	7 N 14.007	8 O 16.00	9 F 19.00	10 Ne 20.179
11 Na 22.99	12 Mg 24.30											13 Al 26.98	14 Si 28.09	15 P 30.974	16 S 32.06	17 Cl 35.453	18 Ar 39.948
19 K 39.10	20 Ca 40.08	21 Sc 44.96	22 Ti 47.90	23 V 50.94	24 Cr 52.00	25 Mn 54.938	26 Fe 55.85	27 Co 58.93	28 Ni 58.69	29 Cu 63.55	30 Zn 65.39	31 Ga 69.72	32 Ge 72.59	33 As 74.92	34 Se 78.96	35 Br 79.90	36 Kr 83.80
37 Rb 85.47	38 Sr 87.62	39 Y 88.91	40 Zr 91.22	41 Nb 92.91	42 Mo 95.94	43 Tc (98)	44 Ru 101.1	45 Rh 102.91	46 Pd 106.42	47 Ag 107.87	48 Cd 112.41	49 In 114.82	50 Sn 118.71	51 Sb 121.75	52 Te 127.60	53 I 126.91	54 Xe 131.29
55 Cs 132.91	56 Ba 137.33	57 *La 138.91	72 Hf 178.49	73 Ta 180.95	74 W 183.85	75 Re 186.21	76 Os 190.2	77 Ir 192.2	78 Pt 195.08	79 Au 196.97	80 Hg 200.59	81 Tl 204.38	82 Pb 207.2	83 Bi 208.98	84 Po (209)	85 At (210)	86 Rn (222)
87 Fr (223)	88 Ra 226.02	89 †Ac 227.03	104 Rf (261)	105 Db (262)	106 Sg (266)	107 Bh (264)	108 Hs (277)	109 Mt (268)	110 Ds (271)	111 Rg (272)	112 § (277)						

§Not yet named

*Lanthanide Series

58 Ce 140.12	59 Pr 140.91	60 Nd 144.24	61 Pm (145)	62 Sm 150.4	63 Eu 151.97	64 Gd 157.25	65 Tb 158.93	66 Dy 162.50	67 Ho 164.93	68 Er 167.26	69 Tm 168.93	70 Yb 173.04	71 Lu 174.97

†Actinide Series

90 Th 232.04	91 Pa 231.04	92 U 238.03	93 Np 237.05	94 Pu (244)	95 Am (243)	96 Cm (247)	97 Bk (247)	98 Cf (251)	99 Es (252)	100 Fm (257)	101 Md (258)	102 No (259)	103 Lr (262)

CHEMISTRY TEST

Note: For all questions involving solutions, assume that the solvent is water unless otherwise stated.

Throughout the test the following symbols have the definitions specified unless otherwise noted.

H = enthalpy	atm	= atmosphere(s)
M = molar	g	= gram(s)
n = number of moles	J	= joule(s)
P = pressure	kJ	= kilojoule(s)
R = molar gas constant	L	= liter(s)
S = entropy	mL	= milliliter(s)
T = temperature	mm	= millimeter(s)
V = volume	mol	= mole(s)
	V	= volt(s)

Part A

Directions: Each set of lettered choices below refers to the numbered statements or questions immediately following it. Select the one lettered choice that best fits each statement or answers each question and then fill in the corresponding circle on the answer sheet. A choice may be used once, more than once, or not at all in each set.

Questions 1-4 refer to the elements for which the ground-state electron configurations are shown below.

(A) $1s^2\, 2s^1$

(B) $1s^2\, 2s^2$

(C) $1s^2\, 2s^2 2p^2$

(D) $1s^2\, 2s^2 2p^5$

(E) $1s^2\, 2s^2 2p^6$

1. The configuration of the element with the largest second ionization energy

2. The configuration of the element whose atoms are most likely to form four covalent bonds

3. The configuration of the element most likely to form diatomic molecules of the form X_2

4. The configuration of the element that exists as single gaseous atoms at 0°C and 1 atm

Questions 5-7 refer to the following.

(A) White precipitate
(B) Blue precipitate
(C) Orange precipitate
(D) Gas bubbles
(E) No change

5. Observed when concentrated hydrochloric acid is added to calcium carbonate

6. Observed when sodium sulfate solution is added to barium chloride solution

7. Observed when sodium chloride solution is added to potassium nitrate solution

GO ON TO THE NEXT PAGE

Questions 8-10 are based on the following heating curve for a pure substance. The substance begins as a solid and ends as a gas; each segment represents a different process.

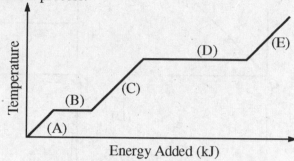

8. Boiling

9. Melting

10. A gas is heated.

GO ON TO THE NEXT PAGE

Questions 11-14 refer to the following graphs.

(A)
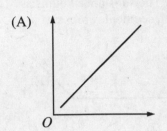

(B)
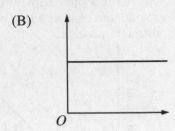

(C)
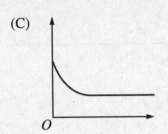

(D)
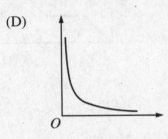

(E)
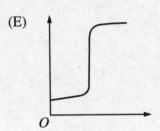

11. Which graph could represent the pH of a $0.1\ M$ solution of nitric acid *versus* the volume of a $0.1\ M$ solution of sodium hydroxide that is added to it?

12. Which graph could represent the concentration of one reactant *versus* time as a reaction approaches and reaches equilibrium?

13. Which graph could represent the pressure of a sample of an ideal gas *versus* its absolute temperature at constant volume?

14. Which graph could represent the product of pressure times volume, *PV*, for an ideal gas *versus* its pressure at constant temperature?

GO ON TO THE NEXT PAGE

Questions 15-17 refer to the following types of substances.

    (A) Hydride
    (B) Halide
    (C) Hydroxide
    (D) Hydrate
    (E) Hydrocarbon

15. A crystalline substance in which water is one of the structural units

16. A compound that contains only a metal and hydrogen

17. An organic compound

Questions 18-19 refer to the following substances at room temperature.

    (A) CO_2
    (B) N_2O
    (C) NO_2
    (D) SiO_2
    (E) CaO

18. Is an ionic solid

19. Is a gas in which each molecule has an unpaired electron

Questions 20-22

    (A) Oxidation
    (B) Decomposition
    (C) Precipitation
    (D) Acid-base
    (E) Reduction

Which of the above best describes the reaction represented by each of the following equations?

20. $CaCO_3(s) \rightarrow CaO(s) + CO_2(g)$

21. $Pb^{2+}(aq) + 2\,I^-(aq) \rightarrow PbI_2(s)$

22. $Fe^{2+}(aq) \rightarrow Fe^{3+}(aq) + e^-$

GO ON TO THE NEXT PAGE

Questions 23-25 refer to the following energy diagram.

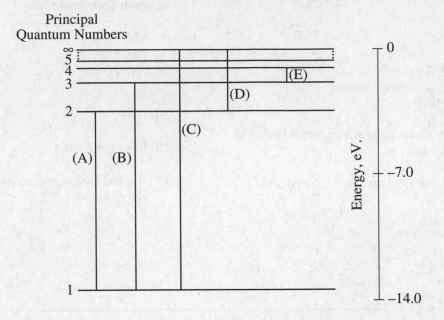

The diagram above is a plot of the energy levels for the electron of the hydrogen atom (roughly to scale) according to the Bohr theory. The vertical lines represent possible transitions (increases or decreases of energy) that can occur.

23. The transition from the ground state to the first excited state of hydrogen

24. Of the transitions shown, the one that involves the LEAST energy

25. The transition that represents the ionization energy of hydrogen

GO ON TO THE NEXT PAGE

PLEASE GO TO THE SPECIAL SECTION AT THE LOWER LEFT-HAND CORNER OF THE PAGE OF THE ANSWER SHEET YOU ARE WORKING ON AND ANSWER QUESTIONS 101-115 ACCORDING TO THE FOLLOWING DIRECTIONS.

Part B

Directions: Each question below consists of two statements, I in the left-hand column and II in the right-hand column. For each question, determine whether statement I is true or false <u>and</u> whether statement II is true or false and fill in the corresponding T or F circles on your answer sheet. <u>Fill in circle CE only if statement II is a correct explanation of the true statement I.</u>

	EXAMPLES:			
	I			**II**
EX 1.	H_2SO_4 is a strong acid	BECAUSE		H_2SO_4 contains sulfur.
EX 2.	An atom of oxygen is electrically neutral	BECAUSE		an oxygen atom contains an equal number of protons and electrons.

SAMPLE ANSWERS

	I		II		CE*
EX1	●	Ⓕ	●	Ⓕ	○
EX2	●	Ⓕ	●	Ⓕ	●

<u>I</u>		<u>II</u>
101. The volume of a gas at constant pressure increases with increasing temperature	BECAUSE	the average speed of gas molecules decreases with increasing temperature.
102. A 1 *M* solution of sodium hydroxide has a high pH	BECAUSE	solutions with a high H^+ concentration have a high pH.
103. H_2S is a polar substance	BECAUSE	H_2S is a gas at room temperature.
104. In its ground state, a magnesium atom has more electrons in its outer shell than does a potassium atom	BECAUSE	the total number of electrons in a magnesium atom is greater than the total number of electrons in a potassium atom.
105. Liquid water in an open container evaporates	BECAUSE	some molecules at the surface of liquid water in an open container have enough kinetic energy to overcome intermolecular attractions.
106. Metallic copper is an electrical conductor	BECAUSE	in metallic copper, the atoms of copper are covalently bonded.
107. Acetic acid, $HC_2H_3O_2$, is a stronger acid than sulfuric acid	BECAUSE	acetic acid has more hydrogen atoms in its molecular structure than does sulfuric acid.

GO ON TO THE NEXT PAGE ▷

I		II

108. Under identical conditions, $N_2(g)$ is more chemically reactive than $O_2(g)$ — **BECAUSE** — the $N_2(g)$ molecule has a single bond and the $O_2(g)$ molecule has a double bond.

109. To prepare a 1 *M* solution of chloride ions from $CaCl_2$ (molar mass 110 g/mol), 110 g of $CaCl_2$ should be dissolved in 1 L of solution — **BECAUSE** — each mole of $CaCl_2$ dissolves to produce 1 mol of chloride ions.

110. The first ionization energy of K is greater than that of Li — **BECAUSE** — the Li atom has a smaller radius than the K atom.

111. Catalysts increase the rates of chemical reactions — **BECAUSE** — the activation energy of a reaction is lowered by a catalyst for the reaction.

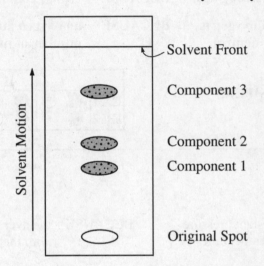

112. In the paper chromatography experiment represented above, component 1 moved up fastest — **BECAUSE** — in the paper chromatography experiment represented above, component 1 moved a shorter distance up the paper than component 2 or 3 did.

113. The boiling point of water, H_2O, is much higher than that of methane, CH_4, — **BECAUSE** — the molar mass of water is greater than that of methane.

$$2\,C_2H_6(g) + 7\,O_2(g) \rightarrow 4\,CO_2(g) + 6\,H_2O(l)$$

114. For the reaction represented by the equation above, the entropy increases as the products form — **BECAUSE** — in the reaction represented above, there are more moles of products than of reactants.

115. At 25°C, the average speed of $H_2(g)$ molecules is less than the average speed of $O_2(g)$ molecules — **BECAUSE** — at 25°C, the average kinetic energy of $H_2(g)$ molecules is less than the average kinetic energy of $O_2(g)$ molecules.

RETURN TO THE SECTION OF YOUR ANSWER SHEET YOU STARTED FOR CHEMISTRY AND ANSWER QUESTIONS 26-70.

GO ON TO THE NEXT PAGE

Part C

Directions: Each of the questions or incomplete statements below is followed by five suggested answers or completions. Select the one that is best in each case and then fill in the corresponding circle on the answer sheet.

26. The oxidation number of S in SO_3 is

    (A) +2
    (B) +3
    (C) +4
    (D) +5
    (E) +6

$$C_3H_8(g) + 5 O_2(g) \rightarrow 3 CO_2(g) + 4 H_2O(g)$$

27. How many moles of water would be produced if 11.0 g of propane (molar mass 44 g/mol) were burned completely to carbon dioxide and water according to the equation represented above?

    (A) 1.0 mol
    (B) 2.0 mol
    (C) 3.0 mol
    (D) 4.0 mol
    (E) 5.0 mol

$$Zn(s) + 2 Ag^+(aq) \rightarrow Zn^{2+}(aq) + 2 Ag(s)$$

28. Which of the following is true of the reaction represented above?

    (A) $Zn(s)$ is the oxidizing agent.
    (B) $Ag^+(aq)$ is the oxidizing agent.
    (C) $Zn(s)$ is reduced.
    (D) $Ag^+(aq)$ is oxidized.
    (E) A mole of electrons is transferred for each 0.5 mol of $Ag(s)$ produced.

$$\ldots NH_3(g) + \ldots O_2(g) \rightarrow \ldots N_2(g) + \ldots H_2O(g)$$

29. When the equation for the reaction represented above is balanced with all the coefficients reduced to the lowest whole-number terms, the coefficient for $O_2(g)$ is

    (A) 1
    (B) 2
    (C) 3
    (D) 4
    (E) 6

30. When 0.0025 mol of HCl and 0.0035 mol of NaOH are added to water to make 1 L of solution, the pH of the resulting solution is approximately

    (A) 1
    (B) 3
    (C) 7
    (D) 11
    (E) 14

31. Which of the following molecules is polar?

    (A) Cl_2
    (B) C_2H_6
    (C) NH_3
    (D) CO_2
    (E) CCl_4

32. An atom of which of the following elements has the greatest number of valence electrons?

    (A) Iodine
    (B) Arsenic
    (C) Barium
    (D) Oxygen
    (E) Carbon

33. Which of the following contains the greatest number of atoms?

    (A) 1.0 g of Fe
    (B) 1.0 g of U
    (C) 1.0 g of Li
    (D) 1.0 g of S
    (E) 1.0 g of C

34. What is the maximum mass of Al (molar mass 27 g/mol) that can be obtained from 20.4 g of pure Al_2O_3 (molar mass 102 g/mol) ?

    (A) 2.70 g
    (B) 5.40 g
    (C) 8.10 g
    (D) 10.8 g
    (E) 16.3 g

GO ON TO THE NEXT PAGE

35. Of the following solutions, which has the highest boiling point?

(A) 0.1 M sucrose, $C_{12}H_{22}O_{11}$
(B) 0.1 M acetic acid, $HC_2H_3O_2$
(C) 0.1 M NaCl
(D) 0.1 M $CaCl_2$
(E) 0.1 M $AlCl_3$

$$2\,A(g) + B(g) \rightleftarrows C(g) + D(g)$$

36. Which of the following is likely to have the smallest effect on the equilibrium concentrations of reactants and products in the gas-phase reaction represented above?

(A) Decreasing the temperature of the system by 25°C
(B) Decreasing the volume of the system by half
(C) Removing one of the products of the reaction from the system
(D) Doubling the amount of one of the reactants in the system
(E) Adding a small amount of a catalyst for the reaction to the system

37. Of the following, the conditions under which the molar volume of gaseous helium is greatest are

(A) 237 K and 1 atm
(B) 300 K and 1 atm
(C) 400 K and 1 atm
(D) 500 K and 2 atm
(E) 600 K and 2 atm

38. How many grams of $RbNO_3$ (molar mass 147 g/mol) are required to produce 0.500 L of a 0.200 M $RbNO_3$ solution?

(A) 73.5 g
(B) 29.6 g
(C) 14.7 g
(D) 2.96 g
(E) 1.47 g

39. SiO_2 has a high melting point because its solid state structure is

(A) ionic
(B) metallic
(C) hydrogen bonded
(D) nonpolar covalent molecular
(E) covalent network

$$\ldots Pb(NO_3)_2(s) \rightarrow \ldots PbO(s) + \ldots NO_2(g) + \ldots O_2(g)$$

40. When the equation above is balanced and all coefficients are reduced to lowest whole-number terms, the coefficient for $NO_2(g)$ is

(A) 2
(B) 4
(C) 6
(D) 8
(E) 10

GO ON TO THE NEXT PAGE

41. Which of the following solutions has the lowest $[H^+]$?

    (A) 0.10 M HNO_2

    (B) 0.10 M HNO_3

    (C) 0.10 M H_2SO_4

    (D) 0.10 M HCl

    (E) 0.10 M HBr

42. At 4°C, a 10. mL container filled with water has a mass of 35.6 g. The same container filled with methanol has a mass of 33.5 g. What is the approximate density of methanol? (The density of water at 4°C is 1.00 g/mL.)

    (A) 0.79 g/mL
    (B) 1.0 g/mL
    (C) 1.3 g/mL
    (D) 2.1 g/mL
    (E) 3.3 g/mL

43. Compounds that have the empirical formula CH include which of the following?

    I. $H_2C{=}CH_2$

    II. $HC{\equiv}CH$

    III.

    $$
    \begin{array}{c}
    H \\
    C \\
    HC \quad\quad CH \\
    \\
    HC \quad\quad CH \\
    C \\
    H
    \end{array}
    $$

    (A) I only
    (B) III only
    (C) I and II only
    (D) II and III only
    (E) I, II, and III

44. The Fe^{3+} ion contains how many electrons?

    (A) 23
    (B) 26
    (C) 29
    (D) 31
    (E) 53

45. The formula for the chloride of radium is

    (A) RaCl
    (B) $RaCl_2$
    (C) $RaCl_3$
    (D) Ra_2Cl
    (E) Ra_2Cl_3

46. A sample of $H_2(g)$ is stored in a 0.500 L vessel at 90.0 torr and 300. K. The gas is transferred to a 1.50 L vessel at constant temperature. Which of the following statements about the gas is correct?

    (A) The number of moles of $H_2(g)$ increases.

    (B) The number of moles of $H_2(g)$ decreases.

    (C) The pressure of the $H_2(g)$ increases to 270. torr.

    (D) The pressure of the $H_2(g)$ decreases to 30.0 torr.

    (E) The pressure of the $H_2(g)$ remains unchanged.

47. How many moles of $O_2(g)$ are formed when a 6.0 mol sample of $KClO_3(s)$ decomposes completely to produce $O_2(g)$ and KCl(s) ?

    (A) 1.5 mol
    (B) 3.0 mol
    (C) 6.0 mol
    (D) 9.0 mol
    (E) 12 mol

GO ON TO THE NEXT PAGE

$$C \text{ (graphite)} + O_2(g) \rightarrow CO_2(g) \qquad \Delta H = -394 \text{ kJ}$$

$$C \text{ (diamond)} + O_2(g) \rightarrow CO_2(g) \qquad \Delta H = -396 \text{ kJ}$$

48. On the basis of the information above, what is the change in enthalpy, ΔH, for the following reaction?

$$C \text{ (graphite)} \rightarrow C \text{ (diamond)}$$

   (A) −790 kJ
   (B)   −4 kJ
   (C)   −2 kJ
   (D)   +2 kJ
   (E) +790 kJ

$$\ldots Zn(s) + \ldots NaOH(aq) + \ldots H_2O(l) \rightarrow \ldots Na_2Zn(OH)_4(aq) + \ldots H_2(g)$$

49. When the equation above is balanced and all coefficients are reduced to lowest whole-number terms, the coefficient for $H_2O(l)$ is

   (A) 1
   (B) 2
   (C) 3
   (D) 4
   (E) 5

GO ON TO THE NEXT PAGE

CHEMISTRY TEST—Continued

50. Which of the following best describes the type of bonding between iodine atoms in a molecule of I_2 ?

(A) Ionic bonding
(B) Metallic bonding
(C) Hydrogen bonding
(D) Covalent bonding
(E) Dispersion (London) force interactions

51. When Na_2SO_4 dissolves in water, which of the following species is present in the greatest concentration in the solution?

(A) $Na^+(aq)$
(B) $Na_2SO_4(aq)$
(C) $SO_4^{2-}(aq)$
(D) $S^{2-}(aq)$
(E) $O^{2-}(aq)$

52. Which of the following statements is true of a solution of 0.10 M HCl(aq) ?

(A) The pH is 1.
(B) The concentration of $Cl^-(aq)$ is greater than the concentration of $H^+(aq)$.
(C) The concentration of $Cl^-(aq)$ is equal to the concentration of $OH^-(aq)$.
(D) The concentration of $H^+(aq)$ is equal to the concentration of $OH^-(aq)$.
(E) The indicator phenolphthalein turns pink when added to the acid solution.

53. The half-life for the radioactive decay of $^{239}_{94}Pu$ is 25,000 years. If 100. g of $^{239}_{94}Pu$ are present initially, how many grams of $^{239}_{94}Pu$ will remain after 50,000 years?

(A) 100. g
(B) 50.0 g
(C) 25.0 g
(D) 12.5 g
(E) 0.000 g

I   II   III

54. Which of the formulas above represent isomers of one another?

(A) None
(B) I and II only
(C) I and III only
(D) II and III only
(E) I, II, and III

55. Which of the following is always characteristic of an oxidizing agent?

(A) It contains oxygen.
(B) It is soluble in water.
(C) It contains a transition element.
(D) It can be reduced.
(E) It forms an ionic lattice.

56. Which of the following statements about a liquid that evaporates readily at room temperature is correct?

(A) It has strong intermolecular forces.
(B) It has a high vapor pressure.
(C) It is considered to be nonvolatile.
(D) It would make its container feel warm to the touch.
(E) It should be stored in an open container.

GO ON TO THE NEXT PAGE

$$H_2(g) + Br_2(g) \rightleftarrows 2\,HBr(g)$$

57. Which of the following is an appropriate expression for the equilibrium constant of the reaction represented above?

(A) $K_c = \dfrac{[H][Br]}{[HBr]}$

(B) $K_c = \dfrac{[H_2][Br_2]}{[HBr]}$

(C) $K_c = \dfrac{[HBr]}{[H_2][Br_2]}$

(D) $K_c = \dfrac{[HBr]^2}{[H_2][Br_2]}$

(E) $K_c = \dfrac{[HBr]^2}{[H]^2[Br]^2}$

58. Atoms with high first ionization energies always have

(A) relatively tightly bound outermost electrons
(B) multiple oxidation states
(C) low electronegativities
(D) large atomic radii
(E) distinctly metallic properties

59. Substances that can act both as an acid and as a base in aqueous solution include which of the following?

  I. Cl^-
  II. HSO_4^-
  III. CO_3^{2-}

(A) I only
(B) II only
(C) III only
(D) I and II only
(E) II and III only

$$\ldots\,C_2H_5OH(l) + \ldots\,O_2(g) \rightarrow \ldots\,CO_2(g) + \ldots\,H_2O(g)$$

60. When the combustion reaction represented by the equation above is balanced using the lowest whole-number coefficients, what is the coefficient of $O_2(g)$?

(A) 2
(B) 3
(C) 4
(D) 5
(E) 6

GO ON TO THE NEXT PAGE

61. When 28 g of Fe reacts as completely as possible with 8.0 g of S to form FeS, which of the following is true?

    (A) Approximately 4.0 g of S remains unreacted.
    (B) Approximately 14 g of Fe remains unreacted.
    (C) Approximately equal masses of Fe and S react.
    (D) Approximately 27 g of FeS is produced.
    (E) Approximately 36 g of FeS is produced.

62. A 9.0 g sample of liquid water has which of the following?

    I. 1.0 mol of hydrogen atoms
    II. 8.5 g of oxygen
    III. A volume of 11.2 L at standard temperature and pressure

    (A) I only
    (B) II only
    (C) III only
    (D) I and II only
    (E) I, II, and III

63. How much energy is required to heat 100. g of H_2O from 20.0°C to 40.0°C ? (The specific heat of $H_2O(l)$ is 4.18 J/(g·°C).)

    (A)   93.6 J
    (B)   482 J
    (C) 2,000 J
    (D) 4,180 J
    (E) 8,360 J

64. If a student were to accurately analyze a mixture of solid NaCl and solid NaOH by titration of the hydroxide ion with a standardized solution of HCl, which of the following would be LEAST useful?

    (A) Bunsen burner
    (B) Analytical balance
    (C) Buret
    (D) Erlenmeyer flask
    (E) Indicator

$$H_2(g) + Cl_2(g) \rightarrow 2\,HCl(g) \qquad \Delta H = -185\ kJ$$

65. According to the equation for the reaction represented above, what is ΔH for the production of 0.100 mol of HCl(g) ?

    (A) −37.0 kJ
    (B) −18.5 kJ
    (C) −9.25 kJ
    (D) +9.25 kJ
    (E) +18.5 kJ

$$2\,SO_2(g) + O_2(g) \rightleftarrows 2\,SO_3(g) + heat$$

66. For the system represented above, which of the following actions will shift the position of equilibrium to the left?

    (A) Increasing the pressure
    (B) Increasing the temperature
    (C) Putting the mixture in a smaller container
    (D) Adding some $O_2(g)$
    (E) Removing some $SO_3(g)$

67. When Na(s) reacts with excess $H_2O(l)$, products of the reaction include which of the following?

    I. $Na^+(aq)$
    II. $OH^-(aq)$
    III. $H_2(g)$

    (A) I only
    (B) III only
    (C) I and II only
    (D) I and III only
    (E) I, II, and III

68. When the following air pollutants are present in small amounts, which is LEAST hazardous to humans?

    (A) Ammonia, NH_3
    (B) Carbon dioxide, CO_2
    (C) Sulfur dioxide, SO_2
    (D) Nitrogen dioxide, NO_2
    (E) Hydrogen sulfide, H_2S

GO ON TO THE NEXT PAGE

69. A compound containing only carbon and hydrogen is found to have a molar mass of 100 g/mol and to consist of 16 percent hydrogen by mass. The number of carbon atoms in one molecule of the compound is

(A) 1
(B) 3
(C) 4
(D) 6
(E) 7

70. A 21 g sample of $NaF(s)$ (molar mass 42 g/mol) is dissolved in enough water to yield 2.0 L of solution. What is the molar concentration of $Na^+(aq)$?

(A) 0.010 *M*
(B) 0.050 *M*
(C) 0.10 *M*
(D) 0.25 *M*
(E) 0.50 *M*

S T O P

**IF YOU FINISH BEFORE TIME IS CALLED, YOU MAY CHECK YOUR WORK ON THIS TEST ONLY.
DO NOT TURN TO ANY OTHER TEST IN THIS BOOK.**

How to Score the SAT Subject Test in Chemistry

When you take an actual SAT Subject Test in Chemistry, your answer sheet will be "read" by a scanning machine that will record your response to each question. Then, a computer will compare your answers with the correct answers and produce your raw score. You get one point for each correct answer. For each wrong answer, you lose one-fourth of a point. Questions you omit (and any for which you mark more than one answer) are not counted. This raw score is converted to a scaled score that is reported to you and to the colleges you specify.

Worksheet 1. Finding Your Raw Test Score

STEP 1: Table A on the following page lists the correct answers for all the questions on the Subject Test in Chemistry that is reproduced in this book. It also serves as a worksheet for you to calculate your raw score.

- Compare your answers with those given in the table.

- Put a check in the column marked "Right" if your answer is correct.

- Put a check in the column marked "Wrong" if your answer is incorrect.

- Leave both columns blank if you omitted the question.

STEP 2: Count the number of right answers.

Enter the total here: _____

STEP 3: Count the number of wrong answers.

Enter the total here: _____

STEP 4: Multiply the number of wrong answers by .250.

Enter the product here: _____

STEP 5: Subtract the result obtained in Step 4 from the total you obtained in Step 2.

Enter the result here: _____

STEP 6: Round the number obtained in Step 5 to the nearest whole number.

Enter the result here: _____

The number you obtained in Step 6 is your raw score.

Answers to Practice Test 1

Table A
Answers to the Subject Test in Chemistry - Practice Test 1 and Percentage of Students Answering Each Question Correctly

Question Number	Correct Answer	Right	Wrong	Percent Answering Correctly*	Question Number	Correct Answer	Right	Wrong	Percent Answering Correctly*
1	A			49	26	E			84
2	C			85	27	A			83
3	D			81	28	B			78
4	E			77	29	C			93
5	D			53	30	D			51
6	A			42	31	C			76
7	E			49	32	A			74
8	D			82	33	C			70
9	B			80	34	D			56
10	E			94	35	E			40
11	E			60	36	E			67
12	C			77	37	C			65
13	A			66	38	C			67
14	B			35	39	E			50
15	D			66	40	B			71
16	A			49	41	A			52
17	E			89	42	A			47
18	E			85	43	D			74
19	C			51	44	A			87
20	B			93	45	B			88
21	C			79	46	D			77
22	A			82	47	D			77
23	A			71	48	D			62
24	E			82	49	B			68
25	C			35	50	D			72

Table A continued on next page

Table A continued from previous page

Question Number	Correct Answer	Right	Wrong	Percent Answering Correctly*	Question Number	Correct Answer	Right	Wrong	Percent Answering Correctly*
51	A			67	101	T, F			85
52	A			64	102	T, F			73
53	C			81	103	T, T			49
54	B			79	104	T, F			65
55	D			83	105	T, T, CE			83
56	B			61	106	T, F			70
57	D			85	107	F, T			61
58	A			71	108	F, F			59
59	B			59	109	F, F			50
60	B			65	110	F, T			69
61	B			54	111	T, T, CE			84
62	A			34	112	F, T			66
63	E			73	113	T, T			52
64	A			75	114	F, T			54
65	C			66	115	F, F			63
66	B			79					
67	E			40					
68	B			65					
69	E			71					
70	D			83					

* These percentages are based on an analysis of the answer sheets for a random sample of 31,785 students who took the original administration of this test and whose mean score was 666. They may be used as an indication of the relative difficulty of a particular question. Each percentage may also be used to predict the likelihood that a typical Subject Test in Chemistry candidate will answer correctly that question on this edition of this test.

Note: Answer explanations can be found on page 65.

Finding Your Scaled Score

When you take SAT Subject Tests, the scores sent to the colleges you specify are reported on the College Board scale, which ranges from 200 to 800. You can convert your practice test score to a scaled score by using Table B. To find your scaled score, locate your raw score in the left-hand column of Table B; the corresponding score in the right-hand column is your scaled score. For example, a raw score of 30 on this particular edition of the Subject Test in Chemistry corresponds to a scaled score of 560.

Raw scores are converted to scaled scores to ensure that a score earned on any one edition of a particular Subject Test is comparable to the same scaled score earned on any other edition of the same Subject Test. Because some editions of the tests may be slightly easier or more difficult than others, College Board–scaled scores are adjusted so that they indicate the same level of performance regardless of the edition of the test taken and the ability of the group that takes it. Thus, for example, a score of 500 on one edition of a test taken at a particular administration indicates the same level of achievement as a score of 500 on a different edition of the test taken at a different administration.

When you take the SAT Subject Tests during a national administration, your scores are likely to differ somewhat from the scores you obtain on the tests in this book. People perform at different levels at different times for reasons unrelated to the tests themselves. The precision of any test is also limited because it represents only a sample of all the possible questions that could be asked.

Table B
Scaled Score Conversion Table
Subject Test in Chemistry - Practice Test 1

Raw Score	Scaled Score	Raw Score	Scaled Score	Raw Score	Scaled Score
85	800	45	630	5	420
84	800	44	620	4	410
83	800	43	620	3	410
82	800	42	610	2	400
81	800	41	610	1	390
80	800	40	600	0	390
79	800	39	600	−1	380
78	800	38	590	−2	380
77	800	37	590	−3	370
76	800	36	580	−4	360
75	790	35	580	−5	360
74	780	34	580	−6	350
73	780	33	570	−7	350
72	770	32	570	−8	340
71	760	31	560	−9	330
70	760	30	560	−10	330
69	750	29	550	−11	320
68	750	28	550	−12	320
67	740	27	540	−13	310
66	730	26	540	−14	310
65	730	25	530	−15	300
64	720	24	530	−16	290
63	720	23	520	−17	280
62	710	22	520	−18	280
61	710	21	510	−19	270
60	700	20	510	−20	260
59	700	19	500	−21	250
58	690	18	500		
57	690	17	490		
56	680	16	480		
55	680	15	480		
54	670	14	470		
53	670	13	470		
52	660	12	460		
51	660	11	460		
50	650	10	450		
49	650	9	440		
48	640	8	440		
47	640	7	430		
46	630	6	430		

How Did You Do on the Subject Test in Chemistry?

After you score your test and analyze your performance, think about the following questions:

Did you run out of time before reaching the end of the test?

If so, you may need to pace yourself better. For example, maybe you spent too much time on one or two hard questions. A better approach might be to skip the ones you can't answer right away and try answering all the questions that remain on the test. Then, if there's time, go back to the questions you skipped.

Did you take a long time reading the directions?

You will save time when you take the test by learning the directions to the Subject Test in Chemistry ahead of time. Each minute you spend reading directions during the test is a minute that you could use to answer questions.

How did you handle questions you were unsure of?

If you were able to eliminate one or more of the answer choices as wrong and guess from the remaining ones, your approach probably worked to your advantage. On the other hand, making haphazard guesses or omitting questions without trying to eliminate choices could cost you valuable points.

How difficult were the questions for you compared with other students who took the test?

Table A shows you how difficult the multiple-choice questions were for the group of students who took this test during its national administration. The right-hand column gives the percentage of students that answered each question correctly.

A question answered correctly by almost everyone in the group is obviously an easier question. For example, 85 percent of the students answered question 101 correctly. But only 40 percent answered question 35 correctly.

Keep in mind that these percentages are based on just one group of students. They would probably be different with another group of students taking the test.

If you missed several easier questions, go back and try to find out why: Did the questions cover material you haven't yet reviewed? Did you misunderstand the directions?

Answer Explanations

For Practice Test 1

Question 1

Choice (A) is the correct answer. Option (A) represents a lithium atom, option (B) represents a beryllium atom, option (C) represents a carbon atom, option (D) represents a fluorine atom, and option (E) represents a neon atom. For options (B), (C), (D), and (E), the first and second electrons removed are valence electrons. For option (A), the first electron removed is a valence electron, but the second electron removed is a core electron. This second electron is very close to the nucleus compared with the second electron removed from the other +1 ions, so the second ionization energy of lithium is larger than the second-ionization energy of the other elements.

Question 2

Choice (C) is the correct answer. Option (C) represents a carbon atom. Each carbon atom has four valence electrons, and a carbon atom can form covalent bonds with four other atoms. Option (A) represents a lithium atom; Li has a low electronegativity and is likely to form ionic bonds with nonmetals. Option (B) represents a beryllium atom; a Be atom has two valence electrons and can form two covalent bonds. Option (D) represents a fluorine atom; an atom of F has seven valence electrons and can form a covalent bond with only one other atom. Option (E) represents a neon atom. Ne is a noble gas and is inert; thus, it is not likely to form bonds with other atoms.

Question 3

Choice (D) is the correct answer. Option (D) represents an atom of fluorine. Each halogen atom has seven valence electrons. In the elemental form, the halogens are composed of diatomic molecules in which the atoms share one pair of electrons.

Question 4

Choice (E) is the correct answer. The noble gases are composed of single gaseous atoms at 0°C and 1 atm. Option (E) represents an atom of neon, a noble gas. Option (A) represents a lithium atom, option (B) represents a beryllium atom, option (C) represents a carbon atom, and option (D) represents a fluorine atom.

Question 5

Choice (D) is the correct answer. When $HCl(aq)$ is added to $CaCO_3(s)$, a reaction occurs in which the products are $Ca^{2+}(aq)$, $Cl^-(aq)$, $H_2O(l)$, and $CO_2(g)$. The net-ionic equation for the reaction is as follows.

$$2 H^+(aq) + CaCO_3(s) \rightarrow Ca^{2+}(aq) + H_2O(l) + CO_2(g)$$

The $CO_2(g)$ produced will form bubbles.

Question 6

Choice (A) is the correct answer. When a solution containing $SO_4^{2-}(aq)$ is added to a solution containing $Ba^{2+}(aq)$, $BaSO_4(s)$ precipitates due to its low solubility in water. $BaSO_4(s)$ is white. (Compounds of transition metals tend to be colored; Ba is not a transition metal.)

Question 7

Choice (E) is the correct answer. All alkali metal salts are soluble, all nitrates are soluble, and most common chlorides are soluble. Specifically, $NaNO_3$ and KCl are soluble, so no precipitate forms when $NaCl(aq)$ and $KNO_3(aq)$ are combined. No reaction occurs, so no gas is produced. Thus, no change is observed when $NaCl(aq)$ and $KNO_3(aq)$ are combined.

Question 8

Choice (D) is the correct answer. Segment (A) represents a solid being heated, segment (B) represents melting, segment (C) represents a liquid being heated, segment (D) represents boiling, and segment (E) represents a gas being heated. The temperature does not change as a pure substance changes state.

Question 9

Choice (B) is the correct answer. Segment (A) represents a solid being heated, segment (B) represents melting, segment (C) represents a liquid being heated, segment (D) represents boiling, and segment (E) represents a gas being heated. The temperature does not change as a pure substance changes state.

Question 10

Choice (E) is the correct answer. Segment (A) represents a solid being heated, segment (B) represents melting, segment (C) represents a liquid being heated, segment (D) represents boiling, and segment (E) represents a gas being heated.

Question 11

Choice (E) is the correct answer. The curve in option (E) is the shape of a titration curve of an acid titrated with a base, with pH on the vertical axis and volume of base added on the horizontal axis. The pH is low at first and increases as the amount of added base increases. The change in pH is gradual at first, is greatest near the equivalence point of the titration, and then is gradual again.

Question 12

Choice (C) is the correct answer. Concentration is on the vertical axis, and time is on the horizontal axis. As a reaction proceeds, the concentration of the reactants decreases as they are consumed. Once equilibrium is reached, the concentration of the reactants remains constant.

Question 13

Choice (A) is the correct answer. For an ideal gas, $PV = nRT$. P and T are directly proportional; as T increases, P increases, and a graph of P versus T looks like option (A).

Question 14

Choice (B) is the correct answer. For an ideal gas, $PV = nRT$. For a given amount of gas at a constant temperature, as P increases, V decreases, and $(P \times V)$ is constant. PV is on the vertical axis, and P is on the horizontal axis. Since PV is constant at constant temperature, the plot is a horizontal line.

Question 15

Choice (D) is the correct answer. A hydrate (e.g., $CuSO_4 \cdot 5H_2O$) is a salt consisting of a lattice of cations and anions with H_2O molecules incorporated into the lattice structure.

Question 16

Choice (A) is the correct answer. A hydride is a compound that contains the hydride ion, H^-. A compound composed of a metal and hydrogen (e.g., NaH) is a hydride.

Question 17

Choice (E) is the correct answer. Hydrocarbons are composed of only carbon and hydrogen. Hydrocarbons are one of the most familiar types of organic compounds.

Question 18

Choice (E) is the correct answer. When an element that has a low electronegativity combines with an element that has a high electronegativity, an ionic compound forms. Ca is a metal with a low electronegativity, and O is a nonmetal with a high electronegativity. CO_2, N_2O, NO_2, and SiO_2 are each composed of two nonmetals (or a nonmetal and a metalloid) that do not have a large difference in electronegativity, and they thus have covalent bonds. CO_2, N_2O, and NO_2 are gases at room temperature.

Question 19

Choice (C) is the correct answer. A nitrogen atom has five valence electrons, and each oxygen atom has six valence electrons, so an NO_2 molecule has a total of 17 valence electrons. Therefore, it must have an unpaired electron. The other substances all have an even number of electrons and no unpaired electrons.

Question 20

Choice (B) is the correct answer. A decomposition reaction is a reaction in which one substance breaks down into two or more substances.

Question 21

Choice (C) is the correct answer. A precipitation reaction is a reaction in which aqueous ions combine to form a solid ionic compound.

Question 22

Choice (A) is the correct answer. An oxidation reaction is a reaction in which a substance loses one or more electrons, causing its oxidation state to increase.

Question 23

Choice (A) is the correct answer. The level labeled with the principal quantum number of 1 is the ground state for an electron in a hydrogen atom. The level labeled with the principal quantum number of 2 is the first (lowest energy) excited state.

Question 24

Choice (E) is the correct answer. The diagram is roughly to scale; the difference in energy between energy levels with adjacent principal quantum numbers is smaller for higher principal quantum numbers. The transition involving the least energy is the transition between levels 3 and 4.

Question 25

Choice (C) is the correct answer. The ionization energy is the energy required to remove an electron from a gaseous atom in its ground state. This corresponds to the transition from the principal quantum number of 1 to infinity.

Question 26

Choice (E) is the correct answer. The oxidation number of O in compounds is usually −2. This is multiplied by the number of O atoms (3) to get −6, so the oxidation number of S has to be +6 because the SO_3 molecule is neutral (no net charge).

Question 27

Choice (A) is the correct answer. An 11 g sample of propane contains 0.25 mol of propane. According to the balanced chemical equation, for each mole of propane burned, 4 mol of water are produced; 4 times 0.25 is 1.0, so 1.0 mol of water is produced.

Question 28

Choice (B) is the correct answer. In the reaction, $Zn(s)$ is oxidized (it loses electrons and is the reducing agent) and $Ag^+(aq)$ is reduced (it gains electrons and is the oxidizing agent). Because the oxidation number of silver changes from +1 to 0, for each 0.5 mol of $Ag(s)$ produced, 0.5 mol of electrons is transferred. Thus, (E) is false.

Question 29

Choice (C) is the correct answer. There are two nitrogen atoms on the right side of the equation and one on the left side, so a coefficient of 2 should be put in front of the $NH_3(g)$. Then, to balance the H atoms, a coefficient of 3 should be put in front of the $H_2O(g)$. This results in a coefficient of $\frac{3}{2}$ in front of the $O_2(g)$ to balance the O atoms. Each coefficient thus needs to be multiplied by 2 to produce whole-number coefficients, resulting in a coefficient of 3 in front of the $O_2(g)$. The final balanced equation is $4 NH_3(g) + 3 O_2(g) \rightarrow 2 N_2(g) + 6 H_2O(g)$.

Question 30

Choice (D) is the correct answer. An acid-base reaction occurs, with HCl as the limiting reactant. When all of the H^+ reacts with OH^-, (0.0035 mol − 0.0025 mol) = 0.0010 mol of OH^- remains. Because $pOH = -\log[OH^-] = -\log(1.0 \times 10^{-3})$, $pOH = 3$. Since $pH + pOH = 14$, the pH is 11.

Question 31

Choice (C) is the correct answer. Cl_2, C_2H_6, CO_2, and CCl_4 are all nonpolar. Cl_2 is symmetrical. In C_2H_6, CO_2, and CCl_4, the bonds are equivalent, the molecules are symmetrical, and the bond dipoles cancel. The atoms in NH_3 do not lie on the same plane because of the nonbonding pair of electrons on the N atom, so the N–H bond dipoles do not cancel and the molecule is polar.

Question 32

Choice (A) is the correct answer. An iodine atom has seven valence electrons, an arsenic atom has five valence electrons, a barium atom has two valence electrons, an oxygen atom has six valence electrons, and a carbon atom has four valence electrons.

Question 33

Choice (A) is the correct answer. One mole of every element contains 6×10^{23} atoms of the element. The element with the lowest molar mass contains the greatest number of moles $\left(\frac{1 \text{ mol}}{x \text{ g}} \times 1.0 \text{ g} = \frac{1}{x} \text{ mol}\right)$ and thus contains the greatest number of atoms. The molar mass of Li is the lowest of the choices given, 7 g/mol.

Question 34

Choice (D) is the correct answer. A 20.4 g sample of Al_2O_3 is 0.20 mol of Al_2O_3. There are two moles of Al in each mole of Al_2O_3, so 0.40 mol of Al is produced. A 0.40 mol sample of Al has a mass of 10.8 g. Alternatively, a 102 g (one mole) sample of Al_2O_3 contains $2 \times 26.98 = 54.0$ g of Al. By proportion, $\frac{54.0 \text{ g Al}}{102 \text{ g } Al_2O_3} = \frac{x \text{ g Al}}{20.4 \text{ g } Al_2O_3}$, and because the fraction on the left is a little more than one-half, it can be estimated that the mass of Al is a little more than half of 20.4 g.

Question 35

Choice (E) is the correct answer. In aqueous solutions, the increase in boiling point is proportional to the molality multiplied by the number of particles in the solute. Sucrose does not dissociate in aqueous solution. Acetic acid is a weak acid, so it only partially dissociates. NaCl dissociates into two ions, $CaCl_2$ dissociates into three ions, and $AlCl_3$ dissociates into four ions. The difference in the number of particles is significant, so the molarity can be used as a rough estimate of the molality. The molarity is the same in all five options, so because $AlCl_3$ dissociates into the most particles in solution, the $AlCl_3$ solution has the highest boiling point.

Question 36

Choice (E) is the correct answer. The temperature affects the equilibrium constant, so decreasing the temperature will likely change the position of equilibrium. According to Le Châtelier's principle, when a change is imposed on a system at equilibrium, the position of equilibrium will shift to decrease the effect of the change. There are fewer moles of gas on the product side of the equation than on the reactant side, so a decrease in volume will result in the formation of more moles of products. Removing one of the products will shift the equilibrium to the right. Adding more of one of the reactants will also shift the equilibrium to the right. A catalyst increases the rate of a reaction, but it does NOT change the position of equilibrium.

Question 37

Choice (C) is the correct answer. According to the ideal gas law, $PV = nRT$, and for a given n, V is proportional to $\frac{T}{P}$. Option (C) would result in the largest value of $\frac{T}{P}$.

Question 38

Choice (C) is the correct answer. A 0.500 L sample of 0.200 M $RbNO_3$ contains 0.100 mol of $RbNO_3$, which contains 14.7 g of $RbNO_3$.

Question 39

Choice (E) is the correct answer. SiO_2 is a covalent network solid. Each Si atom is connected to four O atoms with relatively strong covalent bonds, and each of the O atoms is bonded to another Si atom. This array, interconnected with strong covalent bonds, requires a large amount of energy to be disrupted, which means that the melting point is high.

Question 40

Choice (B) is the correct answer. There is an even number of oxygen atoms on the left side of the equation, so the coefficient of PbO must be even because there is an even number of O atoms in the other products. If the coefficient of PbO is equal to 2, to balance the Pb atoms, the coefficient of $Pb(NO_3)_2$ must be equal to 2. This results in 4 atoms of N on the left side, so the coefficient of NO_2 is 4. With a coefficient of 1 on O_2, this results in 12 O atoms on each side of the equation. The final balanced equation is 2 $Pb(NO_3)_2(s) \rightarrow$ 2 $PbO(s)$ + 4 $NO_2(g)$ + $O_2(g)$.

Question 41

Choice (A) is the correct answer. All of the options have the same molar concentration, and HNO_3, H_2SO_4, HCl, and HBr are all strong acids. But HNO_2 is a weak acid, so it dissociates the least in aqueous solution and therefore its solution has the lowest H^+ concentration.

Question 42

Choice (A) is the correct answer. The mass of the container filled with methanol is less than the mass of the container filled with water, so the density of methanol must be less than the density of water. The only option less than 1.00 g/mL is option (A). The correct answer can also be calculated. Because the mass of the container and 10. mL of water is 35.6 g, the mass of the container must be 35.6 g − 10. g = 25.6 g. The mass of the 10. mL of methanol is 33.5 g − 25.6 g = 7.9 g. The density of the methanol is thus 7.9 g/10. mL = 0.79 g/mL.

Question 43

Choice (D) is the correct answer. An empirical formula shows the ratio of the numbers of atoms of the different elements in the compound in terms of smallest whole numbers. The molecular formula of compound I is C_2H_4, so its empirical formula is CH_2, not CH. The molecular formula of compound II is C_2H_2, so its empirical formula is CH. The molecular formula of compound III is C_6H_6, so its empirical formula is CH.

Question 44

Choice (A) is the correct answer. An Fe atom has 26 protons and 26 electrons. An atom of Fe loses three electrons to form the ion Fe^{3+}, so the Fe^{3+} ion has $(26 - 3) = 23$ electrons.

Question 45

Choice (B) is the correct answer. Radium, Ra, is an alkaline earth metal, so the radium ion has a charge of +2 in compounds. The chloride ion has a charge of −1. Thus, the formula is $RaCl_2$.

Question 46

Choice (D) is the correct answer. $P_1V_1 = P_2V_2$,

so $P_2 = \dfrac{P_1V_1}{V_2} = \dfrac{(90.0 \text{ torr})(0.500 \text{ L})}{1.50 \text{ L}} = 30.0$ torr. The number of moles of $H_2(g)$ remains constant.

Question 47

Choice (D) is the correct answer. The balanced equation for the decomposition reaction is $2\,KClO_3(s) \rightarrow 2\,KCl(s) + 3\,O_2(g)$. Therefore, when 6.0 mol of $KClO_3(s)$ decomposes, 9.0 mol of $O_2(g)$ forms.

Question 48

Choice (D) is the correct answer. The third equation results when the first equation is added to the reverse of the second equation.

$$C \text{ (graphite)} + O_2(g) \rightarrow CO_2(g) \qquad \Delta H = -394 \text{ kJ}$$

$$CO_2(g) \rightarrow C \text{ (diamond)} + O_2(g) \qquad \Delta H = +396 \text{ kJ}$$

$$\overline{C \text{ (graphite)} \rightarrow C \text{ (diamond)}}$$

When the second equation is reversed, the sign of its ΔH changes. The calculation is $-394 \text{ kJ} + 396 \text{ kJ} = 2 \text{ kJ}$.

Question 49

Choice (B) is the correct answer. There are two Na atoms on the right side of the equation, so a coefficient of 2 should be placed in front of the NaOH(aq). There is an even number of O atoms on the right side of the equation, so a coefficient of 2 should be placed in front of the $H_2O(l)$. The final balanced equation is $Zn(s) + 2\ NaOH(aq) + 2\ H_2O(l) \rightarrow Na_2Zn(OH)_4(aq) + H_2(g)$.

Question 50

Choice (D) is the correct answer. Covalent bonds form between atoms in a compound when there is not a large difference between the electronegativities of the atoms. In this case, the atoms are identical, so the difference in electronegativity is zero and the bonding is covalent.

Question 51

Choice (A) is the correct answer. Na_2SO_4 dissociates into $Na^+(aq)$ ions and $SO_4^{2-}(aq)$ ions in aqueous solution. There are twice as many $Na^+(aq)$ ions as $SO_4^{2-}(aq)$ ions. The species in the other three options do not exist in the solution.

Question 52

Choice (A) is the correct answer. HCl dissociates completely in aqueous solution to produce an equal number of $H^+(aq)$ ions and $Cl^-(aq)$ ions. Because pH = $-log[H^+]$, pH = $-log(1 \times 10^{-1}) = -(-1) = 1$. The solution is acidic, so the concentration of $OH^-(aq)$ is much less than the concentration of $H^+(aq)$ (and thus much less than the concentration of $Cl^-(aq)$). Phenolphthalein is pink in a basic solution, not an acidic solution.

Question 53

Choice (C) is the correct answer. Since the half-life is 25,000 years, 50.0 g of $^{239}_{94}Pu$ remains after 25,000 years and 25.0 g of $^{239}_{94}Pu$ remains after another 25,000 years.

Question 54

Choice (B) is the correct answer. Isomers have the same chemical formula but different structures. The formulas of compounds I, II, and III are $C_2H_2Cl_2$, $C_2H_2Cl_2$, and C_2HCl_3, respectively. In compound I, there are two Cl atoms bonded to the same carbon atom, and in compound II, the two Cl atoms are bonded to different C atoms.

Question 55

Choice (D) is the correct answer. In the course of a redox reaction, oxidizing agents are reduced. They do not necessarily contain oxygen, dissolve in water, contain a transition element, or form an ionic lattice.

Question 56

Choice (B) is the correct answer. The pressure of a vapor over its liquid at equilibrium is the vapor pressure. Liquids that evaporate readily have high vapor pressures. If the liquid evaporates readily, this means that the intermolecular forces between the molecules in the liquid must be relatively weak, and it is easy for the liquid to vaporate. Volatile liquids should be stored in closed containers. Evaporation is an endothermic process, so evaporation may result in the container feeling cool to the touch.

Question 57

Choice (D) is the correct answer. In an equilibrium expression, products are in the numerator and reactants are in the denominator. The molar concentration of each of the gases is raised to a power equal to its coefficient in the balanced equation.

Question 58

Choice (A) is the correct answer. Ionization energy is the energy required to remove an electron from a gaseous atom or ion, so atoms with high first ionization energies must have tightly bound outermost electrons. In a given period of the periodic table, the first ionization energy generally increases from left to right. This means that elements with high first ionization energies are often nonmetals and often have high electronegativities. First ionization energies decrease going down a group of the periodic table, but atomic radius increases. Many of the transition metals have multiple oxidation states but have low first ionization energies. Noble gases have very high first ionization energies but typically have an oxidation state of 0.

Question 59

Choice (B) is the correct answer. A substance that can act as both an acid and a base in aqueous solution can either lose or gain a proton. Neither Cl^- nor CO_3^{2-} can lose a proton in aqueous solution. HSO_4^- can gain a proton (H^+) to form H_2SO_4 and can lose a proton to form SO_4^{2-}.

Question 60

Choice (B) is the correct answer. There are two C atoms on the left side of the equation, so a coefficient of 2 should be put in front of the $CO_2(g)$. There are six H atoms on the left side of the equation, so a coefficient of 3 should be put in front of the $H_2O(g)$. This results in seven O atoms on the right side of the equation. There is one O atom in C_2H_5OH, so the coefficient of $H_2O(g)$ must therefore be 3. The final balance equation is $C_2H_5OH(l) + 3\ O_2(g) \rightarrow 2\ CO_2(g) + 3\ H_2O(g)$.

Question 61

Choice (B) is the correct answer. FeS contains 56 g of Fe for each 32 g of S. All of the S reacts because it is the limiting reactant. Therefore, 8.01g of S reacts with only $\left(\dfrac{8.0}{32}\right) \times 56$ g = 14 g of Fe to form 22 g of FeS, and (28 g − 14 g) = 14 g of Fe remains unreacted.

Question 62

Choice (A) is the correct answer. A 9.0 g sample of water is 0.5 mol of water. A 0.5 mol sample of water contains 1.0 mol of hydrogen atoms (so I is correct) and 0.5 mol of oxygen atoms, which is 8.0 g of oxygen, not 8.5 g of oxygen (so II is not correct). A 9.0 g sample of liquid water has a volume of 9.0 mL (so III is not correct); it is 0.5 mol of water vapor that has a volume of 11.2 L at standard temperature and pressure.

Question 63

Choice (E) is the correct answer. Because $q = mc\Delta T$ (where q is heat, m is mass, c is specific heat, and ΔT is the change in temperature), the calculation is as follows: $q = 100.\ \text{g} \times 4.18\ \text{J/(g} \cdot °\text{C)} \times (40.0°\text{C} - 20.0°\text{C})$ = 8,360 J.

Question 64

Choice (A) is the correct answer. The analytical balance would be used to weigh out the solid sample, which would then be put in an Erlenmeyer flask. An indicator would also be added to the flask. The HCl solution would be put in the buret. There is no use for a Bunsen burner in a titration experiment.

Question 65

Choice (C) is the correct answer. According to the equation, when 2 mol of HCl(g) is produced, $\Delta H = -185$ kJ. Therefore, when 0.100 mol of HCl(g) is produced, $\Delta H = 0.100$ mol HCl $\times \dfrac{-185 \text{ kJ}}{2 \text{ mol HCl}} = -9.25$ kJ.

Question 66

Choice (B) is the correct answer. According to Le Châtelier's principle, when a change is made to a system at equilibrium, the position of equilibrium shifts to decrease the effect of the change. Because the reaction is exothermic, increasing the temperature would shift the equilibrium to the left. Increasing the pressure or putting the mixture in a smaller container would shift equilibrium to the side of the equation with fewer moles of gas (the product side). Adding $O_2(g)$ or removing $SO_3(g)$ would shift equilibrium to the right.

Question 67

Choice (E) is the correct answer. When an alkali metal, M, is put in water, the reaction that occurs is $2\,M(s) + 2\,H_2O(l) \rightarrow 2\,M^+(aq) + 2\,OH^-(aq) + H_2(g)$. Because Na is an alkali metal, I, II, and III are all products of the reaction.

Question 68

Choice (B) is the correct answer. Carbon dioxide is present in Earth's atmosphere at a concentration of approximately 400 ppm, but humans can be exposed to higher concentrations without harm. The other compounds range from being eye and respiratory irritants to being highly toxic at fairly low concentrations.

Question 69

Choice (E) is the correct answer. Because the compound is 16% H and 84% C by mass, it contains 16 H atoms (16 × 1 amu = 16 amu) for every 7 C atoms (7 × 12 amu = 84 amu). Thus, because the molar mass of C_7H_{16} is 100 g/mol, the empirical formula is C_7H_{16}.

Question 70

Choice (D) is the correct answer. If $\frac{1.0 \text{ mol}}{42 \text{ g}} \times 21$ g = 0.50 mol of NaF(s) is used to make 2.0 L of solution, the concentration of NA$^+$ is $\frac{0.50 \text{ mol}}{2.0 \text{ L}}$ = 0.25 M.

Question 101

Choice (T, F) is the correct answer. According to the ideal gas law, $PV = nRT$, V increases with increasing T at constant P, so the first statement is true. The average speed of gas molecules increases (not decreases) with increasing temperature, so the second statement is false.

Question 102

Choice (T, F) is the correct answer. Sodium hydroxide is a strong base, and bases have high pHs, so the first statement is true. Because pH = $-\log[H^+]$, solutions with a high H$^+$ concentration have a low pH, so the second statement is false.

Question 103

Choice (T, T) is the correct answer. The S atom in an H$_2$S molecule has two nonbonding pairs of electrons, so the molecule is bent. This means that the dipoles do not cancel and the molecule is polar, so the first statement is true. H$_2$S is a gas at room temperature, so the second statement is true. The fact that H$_2$S is a gas at room temperature does not explain why H$_2$S is polar, so the second statement is not a correct explanation of the first statement.

Question 104

Choice (T, F) is the correct answer. Magnesium is in the second column of the periodic table, and a magnesium atom has two electrons in its outer shell ($3s^2$). Potassium is in the first column of the periodic table, and a potassium atom has one electron in its outer shell ($4s^1$). Therefore, the first statement is true. The total number of electrons in a magnesium atom is 12, and the total number of electrons in a potassium atom is 19, so the second statement is false.

Question 105

Choice (T, T, CE) is the correct answer. It is true that liquids evaporate when placed in an open container. This is because some of the molecules near the surface have enough kinetic energy to overcome intermolecular attractions with other molecules in the liquid and leave the surface, entering the gas phase. Both statements are true, and the second statement explains the first statement.

Question 106

Choice (T, F) is the correct answer. Copper, like other metals, is a good conductor. Metals have a sea of electrons that are relatively free to move around, so elemental metals are good conductors. Metals have metallic bonding, not covalent bonding, so the second statement is false.

Question 107

Choice (F, T) is the correct answer. Acetic acid is a weak acid; therefore, only a small proportion of the $HC_2H_3O_2$ molecules break apart into H^+ and $C_2H_3O_2^-$ ions. H_2SO_4 is a strong acid. A molecule of $HC_2H_3O_2$ has four H atoms, and an H_2SO_4 molecule has two H atoms, so the second statement is true.

Question 108

Choice (F, F) is the correct answer. $N_2(g)$ is less reactive than $O_2(g)$, so the first statement is false. An $N_2(g)$ molecule has a triple bond and an $O_2(g)$ molecule has a double bond, so the second statement is false.

Question 109

Choice (F, F) is the correct answer. Dissolving 1 mol of $CaCl_2$ in enough water to make 1 L of solution yields 2 mol of Cl^- ions per liter of solution (2 M Cl^-), so both the first statement and the second statement are false.

Question 110

Choice (F, T) is the correct answer. Ionization energy decreases going down a group of the periodic table, so the first statement is false because K is below Li. Atomic radius increases going down a group of the periodic table, so the second statement is true.

Question 111

Choice (T, T, CE) is the correct answer. Catalysts increase the rate of a chemical reaction by providing a pathway with a lower activation energy. Therefore, both statements are true and the second statement is a correct explanation of the first statement.

Question 112

Choice (F, T) is the correct answer. In the chromatography experiment, the sample was put on the original spot on the chromatography paper, then the chromatography paper was placed in a vessel containing a small amount of solvent. The components gradually separated as the solvent carried them up the chromatography paper at different rates. Component 1 moved the shortest distance from the original spot in a given time, so it moved slowest. Therefore, the first statement is false. By observation, the second statement is true.

Question 113

Choice (T, T) is the correct answer. At 25°C and 1 atm, water is a liquid and methane is a gas, so water must have a higher boiling point than methane, and the first statement is true. The molar mass of water (18 g/mol) is greater than that of methane (16 g/mol), so the second statement is true. However, the second statement does not explain the first statement. Water has a higher boiling point than methane because water exhibits hydrogen bonding, whereas methane does not.

Question 114

Choice (F, T) is the correct answer. Gases have much more entropy than liquids or solids. There are 9 mol of gaseous reactants and only 4 mol of gaseous products, so the entropy decreases as the reaction proceeds, and the first statement is false. It is true that there are more moles of products (10) than reactants (9) in the equation, but in this case the 6 mol of $H_2O(l)$ does not contribute significantly to the entropy of the products.

Question 115

Choice (F, F) is the correct answer. At a given temperature, the average kinetic energy is the same for all gases, so the second statement is false. The $H_2(g)$ molecules and $O_2(g)$ molecules have the same average kinetic energy. However, the $H_2(g)$ molecules have less mass. Because the average speed of gas molecules is inversely proportional to the square root of the mass of the molecules, molecules with a lower mass have a higher average speed.

Chemistry Subject Test - Practice Test 2

Practice Helps

The test that follows is an actual, previously administered SAT Subject Test in Chemistry. To get an idea of what it's like to take this test, practice under conditions that are much like those of an actual test administration.

- Set aside an hour when you can take the test uninterrupted.

- Sit at a desk or table with no other books or papers. Dictionaries, other books, or notes are not allowed in the test room.

- Tear out an answer sheet from the back of this book and fill it in just as you would on the day of the test. One answer sheet can be used for up to three Subject Tests.

- Read the instructions that precede the practice test. During the actual administration, you will be asked to read them before answering test questions.

- Time yourself by placing a clock or kitchen timer in front of you.

- After you finish the practice test, read the sections "How to Score the SAT Subject Test in Chemistry" and "How Did You Do on the Subject Test in Chemistry?"

- The appearance of the answer sheet in this book may differ from the answer sheet you see on test day.

CHEMISTRY TEST

The top portion of the page of the answer sheet that you will use to take the Chemistry Test must be filled in exactly as illustrated below. When your supervisor tells you to fill in the circle next to the name of the test you are about to take, mark your answer sheet as shown.

After filling in the circle next to the name of the test you are taking, locate the Background Questions section, which also appears at the top of your answer sheet (as shown above). This is where you will answer the following Background Questions on your answer sheet.

BACKGROUND QUESTIONS

Please answer the four questions below by filling in the appropriate circle in the Background Questions box on your answer sheet. <u>The information you provide is for statistical purposes only and will not affect your test score.</u>

Question I

How many semesters of chemistry have you taken in high school? (If you are taking chemistry this semester, count it as a full semester.) Fill in only <u>one</u> circle of circles 1-3.

- One semester or less   —Fill in circle 1.
- Two semesters   —Fill in circle 2.
- Three semesters or more   —Fill in circle 3.

Question II

How recently have you studied chemistry?

- I am currently enrolled in or have
  just completed a chemistry course.   —Fill in circle 4.
- I have not studied chemistry for
  6 months or more.   —Fill in circle 5.

Question III

Which of the following best describes your preparation in algebra? (If you are taking an algebra course this semester, count it as a full semester.) Fill in only <u>one</u> circle of circles 6-8.

- One semester or less   —Fill in circle 6.
- Two semesters   —Fill in circle 7.
- Three semesters or more   —Fill in circle 8.

Question IV

Are you currently taking Advanced Placement Chemistry? If you are, fill in circle 9.

When the supervisor gives the signal, turn the page and begin the Chemistry Test. There is a total of 85 questions in the Chemistry Test (1-70 plus questions 101-115 that must be answered on the special section at the lower left-hand corner of the answer sheet).

CHEMISTRY TEST

MATERIAL IN THE FOLLOWING TABLE MAY BE USEFUL IN ANSWERING THE QUESTIONS IN THIS EXAMINATION.

PERIODIC TABLE OF THE ELEMENTS

1 H 1.0079																		2 He 4.0026
3 Li 6.941	4 Be 9.012											5 B 10.811	6 C 12.011	7 N 14.007	8 O 16.00	9 F 19.00	10 Ne 20.179
11 Na 22.99	12 Mg 24.30											13 Al 26.98	14 Si 28.09	15 P 30.974	16 S 32.06	17 Cl 35.453	18 Ar 39.948
19 K 39.10	20 Ca 40.08	21 Sc 44.96	22 Ti 47.90	23 V 50.94	24 Cr 52.00	25 Mn 54.938	26 Fe 55.85	27 Co 58.93	28 Ni 58.69	29 Cu 63.55	30 Zn 65.39	31 Ga 69.72	32 Ge 72.59	33 As 74.92	34 Se 78.96	35 Br 79.90	36 Kr 83.80
37 Rb 85.47	38 Sr 87.62	39 Y 88.91	40 Zr 91.22	41 Nb 92.91	42 Mo 95.94	43 Tc (98)	44 Ru 101.1	45 Rh 102.91	46 Pd 106.42	47 Ag 107.87	48 Cd 112.41	49 In 114.82	50 Sn 118.71	51 Sb 121.75	52 Te 127.60	53 I 126.91	54 Xe 131.29
55 Cs 132.91	56 Ba 137.33	57 *La 138.91	72 Hf 178.49	73 Ta 180.95	74 W 183.85	75 Re 186.21	76 Os 190.2	77 Ir 192.2	78 Pt 195.08	79 Au 196.97	80 Hg 200.59	81 Tl 204.38	82 Pb 207.2	83 Bi 208.98	84 Po (209)	85 At (210)	86 Rn (222)
87 Fr (223)	88 Ra 226.02	89 †Ac 227.03	104 Rf (261)	105 Db (262)	106 Sg (266)	107 Bh (264)	108 Hs (277)	109 Mt (268)	110 Ds (271)	111 Rg (272)	112 § (277)						

§Not yet named

*Lanthanide Series	58 Ce 140.12	59 Pr 140.91	60 Nd 144.24	61 Pm (145)	62 Sm 150.4	63 Eu 151.97	64 Gd 157.25	65 Tb 158.93	66 Dy 162.50	67 Ho 164.93	68 Er 167.26	69 Tm 168.93	70 Yb 173.04	71 Lu 174.97
†Actinide Series	90 Th 232.04	91 Pa 231.04	92 U 238.03	93 Np 237.05	94 Pu (244)	95 Am (243)	96 Cm (247)	97 Bk (247)	98 Cf (251)	99 Es (252)	100 Fm (257)	101 Md (258)	102 No (259)	103 Lr (262)

CHEMISTRY TEST

Note: For all questions involving solutions, assume that the solvent is water unless otherwise stated.

Throughout the test the following symbols have the definitions specified unless otherwise noted.

H	=	enthalpy
M	=	molar
n	=	number of moles
P	=	pressure
R	=	molar gas constant
S	=	entropy
T	=	temperature
V	=	volume

atm	=	atmosphere(s)
g	=	gram(s)
J	=	joule(s)
kJ	=	kilojoule(s)
L	=	liter(s)
mL	=	milliliter(s)
mm	=	millimeter(s)
mol	=	mole(s)
V	=	volt(s)

Part A

Directions: Each set of lettered choices below refers to the numbered statements or questions immediately following it. Select the one lettered choice that best fits each statement or answers each question and then fill in the corresponding circle on the answer sheet. A choice may be used once, more than once, or not at all in each set.

Questions 1-3 refer to the following elements.

(A) Chlorine
(B) Sulfur
(C) Bromine
(D) Oxygen
(E) Carbon

1. Is a nonmetal that is a liquid at 25°C and 1 atm

2. Is a good electrical conductor in one of its solid forms at room temperature and 1 atm

3. Ground-state atoms of this element contain electrons in d orbitals.

Questions 4-7

(A) Fission
(B) Neutralization
(C) Nuclear transformation
(D) Oxidation
(E) Reduction

4. The process by which iron oxide is converted to iron

5. The process by which ^{40}K radioactively decays to ^{40}Ar

6. The process by which carbon is converted to carbon dioxide

7. The reaction of an acid with a base

GO ON TO THE NEXT PAGE

Questions 8-12 refer to the following substances at room temperature and 1 atmosphere.

    (A) CH_3OH

    (B) CCl_4

    (C) CO_2

    (D) NaCl

    (E) CH_4

8. Is a polar covalent molecule

9. Is a linear covalent molecule

10. Is an ionic compound

11. Is a gas that gives a weakly acidic solution when added to water

12. Is a nonpolar liquid

Questions 13-16 refer to the following electron configurations.

    (A) $1s^2\ 2s^2\ 2p^3$

    (B) $1s^2\ 2s^2\ 2p^4$

    (C) $1s^2\ 2s^2\ 2p^5$

    (D) $1s^2\ 2s^2\ 2p^6$

    (E) $1s^2\ 2s^2\ 2p^6\ 3s^1$

13. A noble gas configuration

14. Represents the element with the lowest first-ionization energy

15. Represents the element that most easily gains one electron

16. Represents the element that is most easily oxidized

Questions 17-19 refer to the following pH values.

    (A) Equal to 0

    (B) Greater than 0 but less than 7

    (C) Equal to 7

    (D) Greater than 7 but less than 10

    (E) Greater than 10

17. pH of a solution in which $[H^+] = 1.0 \times 10^{-7}\ M$

18. pH of 0.5 L of 0.1 M HNO_3

19. pH of a solution prepared by dissolving 1.0×10^{-5} mol of solid NaOH in enough water to yield 1.0 L of solution

Questions 20-21 refer to the following compounds.

    (A) CCl_2F_2

    (B) CH_4

    (C) SO_2

    (D) Na_3PO_4

    (E) H_2O_2

Select the compound that is primarily implicated in each of the following environmental problems.

20. Formation of acid rain

21. Destruction of the ozone layer

Questions 22-23 refer to the following.

    (A) London dispersion forces

    (B) Metallic bonding

    (C) Hydrogen bonding

    (D) Ion-dipole attraction

    (E) Network covalent bonding

22. Contributes to the high thermal conductivity of copper

23. Accounts for the hardness of diamond

GO ON TO THE NEXT PAGE

PLEASE GO TO THE SPECIAL SECTION AT THE LOWER LEFT-HAND CORNER OF THE PAGE OF THE ANSWER SHEET YOU ARE WORKING ON AND ANSWER QUESTIONS 101-115 ACCORDING TO THE FOLLOWING DIRECTIONS.

Part B

Directions: Each question below consists of two statements, I in the left-hand column and II in the right-hand column. For each question, determine whether statement I is true or false <u>and</u> whether statement II is true or false and fill in the corresponding T or F circles on your answer sheet. <u>Fill in circle CE only if statement II is a correct explanation of the true statement I.</u>

EXAMPLES:		
I		**II**
EX 1. H_2SO_4 is a strong acid	BECAUSE	H_2SO_4 contains sulfur.
EX 2. An atom of oxygen is electrically neutral	BECAUSE	an oxygen atom contains an equal number of protons and electrons.

SAMPLE ANSWERS

	I		II		CE*
EX1	●	(F)	●	(F)	○
EX2	●	(F)	●	(F)	●

I   **II**

101. Baking soda, $NaHCO_3$, can be used to neutralize acids   BECAUSE   the $HCO_3^-(aq)$ ion can function as a base.

102. Metals in Group 1 (alkali metals) are less reactive as their atomic number increases   BECAUSE   within a group, atomic radius decreases as atomic number increases.

103. Gases approach ideal behavior at high temperatures and low pressures   BECAUSE   at high temperatures and low pressures the actual volume of gas molecules and the attractive forces between them become insignificant.

104. Isotopes result when different atoms of the same element have different numbers of protons   BECAUSE   isotopes are atoms of a given element with different masses.

105. Excited gaseous atoms of an element produce a bright-line emission spectrum   BECAUSE   excited electrons in an atom release photons of only certain discrete frequencies as they return to lower energy states.

GO ON TO THE NEXT PAGE

I		II
106. Acetic acid, $HC_2H_3O_2$, is a strong acid	BECAUSE	each molecule of acetic acid contains four hydrogen atoms.
107. When a pure liquid at its boiling point is converted from a liquid to a gas at constant pressure, its temperature remains constant until the change is completed	BECAUSE	when a pure liquid vaporizes, there is a decrease in entropy.
108. At 25°C, the value of K_w for the reaction represented by the equation $2\,H_2O(l) \rightleftarrows H_3O^+(aq) + OH^-(aq)$ is 10^{-14}	BECAUSE	at 25°C, the concentrations of $OH^-(aq)$ and $H_3O^+(aq)$ in pure water are each 10^{-7} mole per liter.
109. In the laboratory, water should never be added to concentrated sulfuric acid	BECAUSE	when water is added to concentrated sulfuric acid, the heat produced may cause the mixture to splatter.
110. The boiling point of a dilute solution of sugar in water is higher than the boiling point of pure water	BECAUSE	the melting point of pure sugar is higher than the melting point of pure water.
111. The energy per mole required for the process $Na(g) \rightarrow Na^+(g) + e^-$ is less than the energy per mole required for the process $Na^+(g) \rightarrow Na^{2+}(g) + e^-$	BECAUSE	the radius of a Na atom is less than the radius of a Na^+ ion.
112. $C_6H_{14}(l)$ is flammable, whereas $H_2O(l)$ is not	BECAUSE	the mass percent of hydrogen is greater in C_6H_{14} than it is in H_2O.
113. Smaller ions form stronger ionic bonds than larger ions with the same charge do	BECAUSE	metal atoms lose electrons more readily than nonmetal atoms do.
114. As the reaction represented by the equation $CaCO_3(s) \rightarrow CaO(s) + CO_2(g)$ occurs, there is an increase in entropy ($\Delta S > 0$)	BECAUSE	solids are more disordered than gases.
115. Raising the temperature generally increases the rate of a chemical reaction involving gases or liquids	BECAUSE	raising the temperature increases the collision frequency and the fraction of collisions that have an energy greater than the activation energy.

RETURN TO THE SECTION OF YOUR ANSWER SHEET YOU STARTED FOR CHEMISTRY AND ANSWER QUESTIONS 24-70.

GO ON TO THE NEXT PAGE

Part C

Directions: Each of the questions or incomplete statements below is followed by five suggested answers or completions. Select the one that is best in each case and then fill in the corresponding circle on the answer sheet.

24. A ground-state atom of which of the following elements has the most valence electrons?

    (A) Aluminum
    (B) Phosphorus
    (C) Oxygen
    (D) Fluorine
    (E) Carbon

25. Which of the following is the complete Lewis electron-dot diagram for NCl_3 ?

    (A) Cl — N — Cl
    　　　　|
    　　　Cl

    (B) Cl — N̈ — Cl
    　　　　|
    　　　Cl

    (C) :C̈l — N̈ — C̈l:
    　　　　|
    　　　:C̈l:

    (D) :C̈l — C̈l — N̈:
    　　　　|
    　　　:C̈l:

    (E) :C̈l — C̈l — C̈l — N̈:

26. A solution that contains 0.60 g of acetic acid (molar mass 60. g/mol) per liter is prepared. The molarity of the solution is

    (A) $1.0\ M$
    (B) $0.60\ M$
    (C) $0.10\ M$
    (D) $0.06\ M$
    (E) $0.010\ M$

27. In the modern periodic table, the elements are arranged in order of increasing

    (A) mass number
    (B) molecular mass
    (C) atomic mass
    (D) atomic radius
    (E) atomic number

28. Which of the following could be used to illustrate the capability of two elements to combine in different ratios?

    (A) CCl_4 and CF_4
    (B) O_2 and O_3
    (C) H_2O and H_2S
    (D) NO_2 and N_2O_4
    (E) FeO and Fe_2O_3

GO ON TO THE NEXT PAGE

$$\ldots\,Na_2CO_3 + \ldots\,HCl \rightarrow \ldots\,NaCl + \ldots\,H_2O + \ldots\,CO_2$$

29. When the equation above is balanced using lowest whole-number coefficients, the coefficient of H_2O is

    (A) 1
    (B) 2
    (C) 3
    (D) 4
    (E) 5

30. Which of the following methods is best for separating and recovering the components of a solution of methyl alcohol and water?

    (A) Sublimation
    (B) Distillation
    (C) Crystallization
    (D) Filtration
    (E) Paper chromatography

31. When 1.0 L of 1.0 M NaOH is diluted to 2.0 L with distilled water, the Na^+ concentration in the final solution is

    (A) 4.0 M
    (B) 2.0 M
    (C) 1.0 M
    (D) 0.50 M
    (E) 0.20 M

32. Equal volumes of different ideal gases at the same pressure and temperature have the same

    (A) mass
    (B) density
    (C) number of neutrons
    (D) number of electrons
    (E) number of gas particles

$$2\,NH_3(g) + 2\,O_2(g) \rightleftarrows N_2O(g) + 3\,H_2O(g)$$

33. Which of the following is the correct expression for the equilibrium constant, K_c, for the reaction represented above?

    (A) $\dfrac{[NH_3] + [O_2]}{[N_2O] + [H_2O]}$

    (B) $\dfrac{[N_2O] + [H_2O]}{[NH_3] + [O_2]}$

    (C) $\dfrac{[N_2O][H_2O]^3}{[NH_3]^2[O_2]^2}$

    (D) $\dfrac{[NH_3]^2[O_2]^2}{[N_2O][H_2O]^3}$

    (E) $\dfrac{[NH_3][O_2]}{[N_2O] + [H_2O]}$

34. Which of the following trends is observed as the atomic number increases in the series of halogens F, Cl, Br, and I ?

    (A) The atomic radius increases.
    (B) The strength as an oxidizing agent increases.
    (C) The electronegativity increases.
    (D) The first ionization energy increases.
    (E) The number of electrons in the outermost (valence) shell increases.

GO ON TO THE NEXT PAGE

$$\ldots \text{Al(OH)}_3(s) + \ldots \text{H}_2\text{SO}_4(aq) \rightarrow \ldots \text{Al}_2(\text{SO}_4)_3(aq) + \ldots \text{H}_2\text{O}(l)$$

35. When the equation above is balanced using the lowest whole-number coefficients, the coefficient for $\text{Al(OH)}_3(s)$ is

    (A) 1
    (B) 2
    (C) 3
    (D) 4
    (E) 5

$$2\,\text{C}_8\text{H}_{18}(l) + 25\,\text{O}_2(g) \rightarrow 16\,\text{CO}_2(g) + 18\,\text{H}_2\text{O}(l)$$

36. Correct statements about the equation for the reaction represented above include which of the following?

    I. For 2 mol of $\text{C}_8\text{H}_{18}(l)$ consumed, 16×44 g of $\text{CO}_2(g)$ is produced.

    II. At the same temperature and pressure, the number of moles of water produced is 18 times the number of moles of $\text{C}_8\text{H}_{18}(l)$ consumed.

    III. The volume of $\text{CO}_2(g)$ produced is greater than the volume of $\text{O}_2(g)$ consumed if both gases are measured at the same temperature and pressure.

    (A) I only
    (B) III only
    (C) I and II only
    (D) II and III only
    (E) I, II, and III

GO ON TO THE NEXT PAGE

37. Of the following, which molecule has at least one multiple bond?

    (A) NH_3
    (B) CO
    (C) CH_4
    (D) C_2H_6
    (E) H_2S

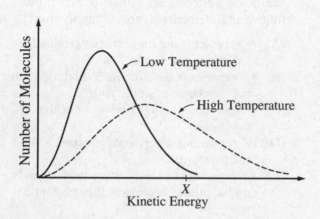

38. The graph above shows the distributions of the kinetic energies of molecules in a sample of gas at two different temperatures. It can be inferred from the graph that at the higher temperature

    (A) the average kinetic energy of the molecules is greater
    (B) the average velocity of the molecules is lower
    (C) there is an increase in the number of molecules
    (D) there are fewer molecules having kinetic energy greater than X
    (E) the forces of attraction among the molecules of the gas are greater

39. Careful heating of a hydrate allows a scientist to determine the chemical formula of the compound. The water in the hydrate is released as water vapor, and the remaining compound is left intact. A copper(II) sulfate hydrate was heated, and the data are shown in the table below. The molar mass of $CuSO_4$ is 160 g/mol.

	Mass
Test tube	12.3 g
Test tube and $CuSO_4$ hydrate	37.3 g
Test tube and $CuSO_4$	28.3 g

Which of the following is the formula of the hydrate?

    (A) $CuSO_4 \cdot H_2O$
    (B) $CuSO_4 \cdot 2H_2O$
    (C) $CuSO_4 \cdot 3H_2O$
    (D) $CuSO_4 \cdot 4H_2O$
    (E) $CuSO_4 \cdot 5H_2O$

40. When copper metal is added to 3 M HNO_3, bubbles of colorless gas are formed. When copper is added to 15 M HNO_3, large amounts of a brown gas are evolved. From these observations alone, it can be concluded that

    (A) hydrogen gas is evolved
    (B) copper can be reduced
    (C) copper does not dissolve in 1 M HNO_3
    (D) some nitric acid is reduced to NH_4^+
    (E) the reaction product depends on the concentration of nitric acid

GO ON TO THE NEXT PAGE

41. Hydrogen bonding would be expected to be an important factor in the interaction of all of the following pairs of molecules EXCEPT

   (A) H_2O and HF
   (B) NH_3 and H_2O
   (C) CH_3OH and NH_3
   (D) B_2H_6 and CH_4
   (E) CH_3OH and HF

$$H_2, \ He, \ O_2, \ CO_2, \ Kr$$

42. Each of five different rigid 1.0 L containers contains a 5.0 g sample of one of the gases listed above at 25°C. The pressure is highest in the container containing which gas?

   (A) H_2
   (B) He
   (C) O_2
   (D) CO_2
   (E) Kr

43. The solubility product constants, K_{sp}, of several carbonates are given below. In a saturated solution of each, which has the lowest concentration of CO_3^{2-} ?

   (A) $MgCO_3$ $K_{sp} = 1.0 \times 10^{-5}$
   (B) $CaCO_3$ $K_{sp} = 4.7 \times 10^{-9}$
   (C) $SrCO_3$ $K_{sp} = 7.0 \times 10^{-10}$
   (D) $ZnCO_3$ $K_{sp} = 2.1 \times 10^{-11}$
   (E) $PbCO_3$ $K_{sp} = 1.5 \times 10^{-13}$

44. What is the maximum number of grams of nitric oxide, NO, that can be produced by combustion of 5.0 mol of nitrogen, N_2 ?

   (A)   15 g
   (B)   30 g
   (C)   50 g
   (D)   150 g
   (E)   300 g

45. A melted crystalline substance is allowed to cool. The graph above shows the temperature of the substance plotted against time. Which of the following statements is most certainly true?

   (A) W represents the highest temperature the substance can reach.
   (B) XY represents the time interval during which the substance is solidifying.
   (C) Z represents the freezing point of the substance.
   (D) YZ represents a period of constant temperature.
   (E) XY represents a temperature that depends on the rate of cooling of the substance.

46. When $NaCl$ is dissolved in pure water at 25°C and 1 atm, the resulting solution, compared to pure water, has a

   (A) lower density
   (B) lower boiling point
   (C) higher freezing point
   (D) higher electrical conductivity
   (E) higher vapor pressure

47. How much heat is required to heat 2.0 g of platinum from 25.0°C to 35.0°C ? (The specific heat capacity of platinum is $0.13 \ \dfrac{J}{g \times °C}$.)

   (A) 0.013 J
   (B) 0.026 J
   (C) 0.26 J
   (D) 1.3 J
   (E) 2.6 J

GO ON TO THE NEXT PAGE

48. Which of the following samples contains the greatest mass of oxygen?

    (A) 0.50 mol of CO
    (B) 0.10 mol of H_2SO_4
    (C) 0.10 mol of $C_6H_{12}O_6$
    (D) 3.0×10^6 molecules of $C_{12}H_{22}O_{11}$
    (E) 3.0×10^{23} molecules of H_2O

$$\ldots Al(s) + \text{excess } S(s) \rightarrow \ldots ?$$

49. How many moles of aluminum are needed to react with excess sulfur, as shown above, in order to form 1 mol of the product?

    (A) 1
    (B) 2
    (C) 3
    (D) 4
    (E) 5

50. The amount of charge that reduces 1.0 mol of Cd^{2+} to Cd metal would also reduce how many moles of Rh^+ to Rh metal?

    (A) 0.50 mol
    (B) 1.0 mol
    (C) 1.5 mol
    (D) 2.0 mol
    (E) 3.0 mol

$$4 Al(s) + 3 O_2(g) \rightarrow 2 Al_2O_3(s)$$

51. When 4.0 mol of $Al(s)$ and 3.0 mol of $O_2(g)$ react according to the equation above, all of the following are possible actual yields of $Al_2O_3(s)$ EXCEPT

    (A) 0.50 mol
    (B) 1.0 mol
    (C) 1.5 mol
    (D) 2.0 mol
    (E) 2.5 mol

52. Which of the following is observed when a small piece of solid zinc is added to an open beaker containing 100 mL of $1\ M\ HCl(aq)$?

    (A) A white precipitate forms and the temperature rises.
    (B) A green precipitate forms and a gas is evolved.
    (C) The zinc disappears and a gas is evolved.
    (D) The solution turns green but no new solid forms.
    (E) Only an increase in the temperature of the solution is observed.

$$\ldots C_4H_{10}(g) + \ldots O_2(g) \rightarrow \ldots CO_2(g) + \ldots H_2O(g)$$

53. When the equation above is balanced and all coefficients are reduced to lowest whole number terms, the coefficient of $CO_2(g)$ is

    (A) 1
    (B) 2
    (C) 4
    (D) 8
    (E) 16

54. Bubbling gaseous hydrogen chloride into distilled water produces a

    (A) precipitate
    (B) basic solution
    (C) solution with $pH < 7$
    (D) solution that does not conduct an electric current
    (E) solution that turns litmus paper blue

GO ON TO THE NEXT PAGE

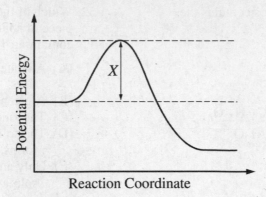

Reaction Coordinate

55. What does the amount of energy represented by the X on the graph represent?

    (A) The midpoint of the reaction
    (B) The potential energy of the products
    (C) The overall energy (enthalpy) of reaction
    (D) The potential energy of the reactants
    (E) The activation energy of the reaction

56. If M represents an alkali metal, the equation for its reaction with excess water is

    (A) $2 \, M(s) + H_2O(l) \rightarrow M_2O(s) + H_2(g)$

    (B) $2 \, M(s) + 2 \, H_2O(l) \rightarrow H_2(g) + 2 \, M^+(aq) + 2 \, OH^-(aq)$

    (C) $M(s) + H_2O(l) \rightarrow MO(s) + H_2(g)$

    (D) $M(s) + 2 \, H_2O(l) \rightarrow H_2(g) + M^{2+}(aq) + 2 \, OH^-(aq)$

    (E) $4 \, M(s) + H_2O(l) \rightarrow 2 \, MH(s) + M_2O(s)$

GO ON TO THE NEXT PAGE

57. Which of the following is an endothermic process?

   (A) $CH_4(g) + 2 O_2(g) \rightarrow CO_2(g) + 2 H_2O(g)$

   (B) $2 Mg(s) + O_2(g) \rightarrow 2 MgO(s)$

   (C) Dilution of concentrated H_2SO_4

   (D) $CO_2(s) \rightarrow CO_2(g)$

   (E) Condensation of a vapor

58. The best way to separate potassium iodide from a mixture of iron filings, sand, and potassium iodide is by

   (A) sublimation
   (B) using a magnet
   (C) extraction with water
   (D) using hydrofluoric acid
   (E) using a sieve

59. The pressure of 2 L of a gas at 27°C is 740 mm Hg. What is the volume of this gas at standard temperature and pressure?

   (A) $V = 2 \times \dfrac{27}{273} \times \dfrac{740}{760}$

   (B) $V = 2 \times \dfrac{273}{300} \times \dfrac{740}{760}$

   (C) $V = 2 \times \dfrac{300}{273} \times \dfrac{740}{760}$

   (D) $V = 2 \times \dfrac{300}{273} \times \dfrac{760}{740}$

   (E) $V = 2 \times \dfrac{273}{300} \times \dfrac{760}{740}$

60. When a few drops of clear $Ba(NO_3)_2$ solution were added to a certain water sample, a precipitate formed. This result provides evidence for the possible presence of which of the following ions in the water sample?

   (A) $Ca^{2+}(aq)$

   (B) $Fe^{2+}(aq)$

   (C) $Cu^{2+}(aq)$

   (D) $Cl^-(aq)$

   (E) $SO_4^{2-}(aq)$

GO ON TO THE NEXT PAGE

$$\ldots C_3H_7OH(g) + \ldots O_2(g) \rightarrow \ldots CO_2(g) + \ldots H_2O(g)$$

61. The combustion of $C_3H_7OH(g)$ is represented by the unbalanced equation above. How many moles of $O_2(g)$ are required to burn 2 mol of $C_3H_7OH(g)$?

    (A) 2 mol
    (B) 6 mol
    (C) 8 mol
    (D) 9 mol
    (E) 10 mol

62. All of the following are oxidation-reduction reactions EXCEPT

    (A) $4 H^+(aq) + 4 Cl^-(aq) + MnO_2(s) \rightarrow Cl_2(g) + MnCl_2(s) + 2 H_2O(l)$
    (B) $C(s) + O_2(g) \rightarrow CO_2(g)$
    (C) $Zn(s) + 2 Ag^+(aq) \rightarrow 2 Ag(s) + Zn^{2+}(aq)$
    (D) $3 Mg(s) + N_2(g) \rightarrow Mg_3N_2(s)$
    (E) $H^+(aq) + OH^-(aq) \rightarrow H_2O(l)$

63. How many milliliters of a $2.0\,M$ HCl solution are required to prepare exactly 1.0 L of a $0.04\,M$ HCl solution?

    (A)   10 mL
    (B)   20 mL
    (C)   40 mL
    (D) 100 mL
    (E) 200 mL

64. A sample of a gas measured at 0°C and 1 atm occupied 1.12 L. The number of molecules it contained was

    (A) $\dfrac{1.12}{6.02 \times 10^{23}}$ molecules

    (B) $0.0500 \, (6.02 \times 10^{23})$ molecules

    (C) $0.500 \, (6.02 \times 10^{23})$ molecules

    (D) $1.12 \, (6.02 \times 10^{23})$ molecules

    (E) $2.24 \, (6.02 \times 10^{23})$ molecules

GO ON TO THE NEXT PAGE

65. For which of the reactions represented below is the change in energy equal to the first ionization energy of Na ?

    (A) $Na^+(g) \rightarrow Na^{2+}(g) + e^-$

    (B) $Na(g) \rightarrow Na^+(g) + e^-$

    (C) $Na(g) \rightarrow Na^{2+}(g) + 2\,e^-$

    (D) $Na(g) + e^- \rightarrow Na^-(g)$

    (E) $Na^-(g) \rightarrow Na^+(g) + 2\,e^-$

66. What is the highest-energy orbital occupied by electrons in the ground state of a chlorine atom?

    (A) $2s$
    (B) $3s$
    (C) $2p$
    (D) $3p$
    (E) $3d$

67. An isotope of element X forms an oxide that is 64 percent oxygen by mass. If the formula of the oxide is XO, what is the atomic mass of X?

    (A)   9.0 amu
    (B) 18 amu
    (C) 25 amu
    (D) 36 amu
    (E) 52 amu

68. At a given temperature and pressure, which of the following gases has the highest rate of effusion through a pinhole?

    (A) H_2
    (B) O_2
    (C) O_3
    (D) H_2O
    (E) H_2O_2

$$K_a = \frac{[H^+][X^-]}{[HX]}$$

69. The expression for the ionization constant, K_a, for the weak acid HX is shown above. If the H^+ concentration is $10^{-3}\,M$ in a $0.10\,M$ solution of the weak acid, what is the value of the ionization constant, K_a ?

    (A) 10^{-1}

    (B) 10^{-3}

    (C) 10^{-5}

    (D) 10^{-6}

    (E) 10^{-7}

$$2\,H_2(g) + O_2(g) \rightarrow 2\,H_2O(g)$$

70. When hydrogen and oxygen react to form water vapor, the heat released is approximately 13 kJ per gram of water formed. The amount of heat evolved when 1 mol of water is formed is approximately

    (A)   1.3 kJ
    (B)   13 kJ
    (C)   26 kJ
    (D) 230 kJ
    (E) 470 kJ

STOP

**IF YOU FINISH BEFORE TIME IS CALLED, YOU MAY CHECK YOUR WORK ON THIS TEST ONLY.
DO NOT TURN TO ANY OTHER TEST IN THIS BOOK.**

How to Score the SAT Subject Test in Chemistry

When you take an actual SAT Subject Test in Chemistry, your answer sheet will be "read" by a scanning machine that will record your response to each question. Then, a computer will compare your answers with the correct answers and produce your raw score. You get one point for each correct answer. For each wrong answer, you lose one-fourth of a point. Questions you omit (and any for which you mark more than one answer) are not counted. This raw score is converted to a scaled score that is reported to you and to the colleges you specify.

Worksheet 1. Finding Your Raw Test Score

STEP 1: Table A on the following page lists the correct answers for all the questions on the Subject Test in Chemistry that is reproduced in this book. It also serves as a worksheet for you to calculate your raw score.

- Compare your answers with those given in the table.

- Put a check in the column marked "Right" if your answer is correct.

- Put a check in the column marked "Wrong" if your answer is incorrect.

- Leave both columns blank if you omitted the question.

STEP 2: Count the number of right answers.

Enter the total here: _____

STEP 3: Count the number of wrong answers.

Enter the total here: _____

STEP 4: Multiply the number of wrong answers by .250.

Enter the product here: _____

STEP 5: Subtract the result obtained in Step 4 from the total you obtained in Step 2.

Enter the result here: _____

STEP 6: Round the number obtained in Step 5 to the nearest whole number.

Enter the result here: _____

The number you obtained in Step 6 is your raw score.

Answers to Practice Test 2

Table A
Answers to the Subject Test in Chemistry - Practice Test 2 and Percentage of Students Answering Each Question Correctly

Question Number	Correct Answer	Right	Wrong	Percent Answering Correctly*	Question Number	Correct Answer	Right	Wrong	Percent Answering Correctly*
1	C			62	26	E			61
2	E			55	27	E			88
3	C			77	28	E			59
4	E			77	29	A			90
5	C			70	30	B			70
6	D			81	31	D			76
7	B			93	32	E			67
8	A			53	33	C			76
9	C			73	34	A			81
10	D			89	35	B			73
11	C			46	36	A			75
12	B			51	37	B			72
13	D			90	38	A			71
14	E			72	39	E			41
15	C			83	40	E			68
16	E			65	41	D			66
17	C			74	42	A			46
18	B			74	43	E			54
19	D			59	44	E			54
20	C			72	45	B			70
21	A			51	46	D			65
22	B			80	47	E			68
23	E			81	48	C			42
24	D			79	49	B			62
25	C			84	50	D			55

Table A continued on next page

Table A continued from previous page

Question Number	Correct Answer	Right	Wrong	Percent Answering Correctly*	Question Number	Correct Answer	Right	Wrong	Percent Answering Correctly*
51	E			62	101	T, T, CE			60
52	C			42	102	F, F			59
53	D			75	103	T, T, CE			53
54	C			73	104	F, T			75
55	E			83	105	T, T, CE			64
56	B			35	106	F, T			57
57	D			48	107	T, F			63
58	C			30	108	T, T, CE			53
59	B			37	109	T, T, CE			60
60	E			44	110	T, T			36
61	D			45	111	T, F			51
62	E			42	112	T, T			45
63	B			60	113	T, T			46
64	B			35	114	T, F			73
65	B			70	115	T, T, CE			83
66	D			69					
67	A			45					
68	A			66					
69	C			38					
70	D			62					

* These percentages are based on an analysis of the answer sheets for a random sample of 8,585 students who took the original administration of this test and whose mean score was 633. They may be used as an indication of the relative difficulty of a particular question. Each percentage may also be used to predict the likelihood that a typical Subject Test in Chemistry candidate will answer correctly that question on this edition of this test.

Note: Answer explanations can be found on page 104.

Finding Your Scaled Score

When you take SAT Subject Tests, the scores sent to the colleges you specify are reported on the College Board scale, which ranges from 200 to 800. You can convert your practice test score to a scaled score by using Table B. To find your scaled score, locate your raw score in the left-hand column of Table B; the corresponding score in the right-hand column is your scaled score. For example, a raw score of 30 on this particular edition of the Subject Test in Chemistry corresponds to a scaled score of 540.

Raw scores are converted to scaled scores to ensure that a score earned on any one edition of a particular Subject Test is comparable to the same scaled score earned on any other edition of the same Subject Test. Because some editions of the tests may be slightly easier or more difficult than others, College Board–scaled scores are adjusted so that they indicate the same level of performance regardless of the edition of the test taken and the ability of the group that takes it. Thus, for example, a score of 500 on one edition of a test taken at a particular administration indicates the same level of achievement as a score of 500 on a different edition of the test taken at a different administration.

When you take the SAT Subject Tests during a national administration, your scores are likely to differ somewhat from the scores you obtain on the tests in this book. People perform at different levels at different times for reasons unrelated to the tests themselves. The precision of any test is also limited because it represents only a sample of all the possible questions that could be asked.

Table B
Scaled Score Conversion Table
Subject Test in Chemistry - Practice Test 2

Raw Score	Scaled Score	Raw Score	Scaled Score	Raw Score	Scaled Score
85	800	45	620	5	410
84	800	44	620	4	400
83	800	43	610	3	400
82	800	42	610	2	390
81	800	41	600	1	390
80	800	40	600	0	390
79	790	39	590	−1	380
78	790	38	590	−2	380
77	780	37	580	−3	370
76	780	36	570	−4	370
75	770	35	570	−5	360
74	770	34	560	−6	360
73	760	33	560	−7	360
72	760	32	550	−8	350
71	750	31	550	−9	350
70	750	30	540	−10	340
69	740	29	540	−11	340
68	740	28	530	−12	330
67	730	27	530	−13	330
66	730	26	520	−14	330
65	720	25	510	−15	320
64	720	24	510	−16	320
63	710	23	500	−17	310
62	710	22	500	−18	310
61	700	21	490	−19	300
60	700	20	490	−20	300
59	690	19	480	−21	290
58	690	18	480		
57	680	17	470		
56	680	16	460		
55	670	15	460		
54	670	14	450		
53	660	13	450		
52	660	12	440		
51	650	11	440		
50	650	10	430		
49	640	9	430		
48	640	8	420		
47	630	7	420		
46	630	6	410		

How Did You Do on the Subject Test in Chemistry?

After you score your test and analyze your performance, think about the following questions:

Did you run out of time before reaching the end of the test?

If so, you may need to pace yourself better. For example, maybe you spent too much time on one or two hard questions. A better approach might be to skip the ones you can't answer right away and try answering all the questions that remain on the test. Then, if there's time, go back to the questions you skipped.

Did you take a long time reading the directions?

You will save time when you take the test by learning the directions to the Subject Test in Chemistry ahead of time. Each minute you spend reading directions during the test is a minute that you could use to answer questions.

How did you handle questions you were unsure of?

If you were able to eliminate one or more of the answer choices as wrong and guess from the remaining ones, your approach probably worked to your advantage. On the other hand, making haphazard guesses or omitting questions without trying to eliminate choices could cost you valuable points.

How difficult were the questions for you compared with other students who took the test?

Table A shows you how difficult the multiple-choice questions were for the group of students who took this test during its national administration. The right-hand column gives the percentage of students that answered each question correctly.

A question answered correctly by almost everyone in the group is obviously an easier question. For example, 84 percent of the students answered question 25 correctly. But only 35 percent answered question 56 correctly.

Keep in mind that these percentages are based on just one group of students. They would probably be different with another group of students taking the test.

If you missed several easier questions, go back and try to find out why: Did the questions cover material you haven't yet reviewed? Did you misunderstand the directions?

Answer Explanations

For Practice Test 2

Question 1

Choice (C) is the correct answer. Bromine is a liquid at 25°C and 1 atm, whereas chlorine and oxygen are gases, and sulfur and carbon are solids.

Question 2

Choice (E) is the correct answer. Diamond and graphite are forms of solid carbon. Graphite is made of layers of honeycomb lattices. Some of the electrons in the lattices are delocalized, making graphite a good conductor of electricity.

Question 3

Choice (C) is the correct answer. Elements with an atomic number of 21 and higher have electrons in d orbitals of their ground-state atoms. Bromine is the only option with an atomic number higher than 21.

Question 4

Choice (E) is the correct answer. Reduction is the gain of electrons, with a decrease in oxidation number. Iron has a positive oxidation number in iron oxide and an oxidation number of 0 in iron metal, so iron gains electrons when iron oxide is converted to iron metal.

Question 5

Choice (C) is the correct answer. Nuclear transformation is the change of an atom of one element to an atom of a different element. Fission involves the splitting of a large nucleus into two smaller nuclei.

Question 6

Choice (D) is the correct answer. Oxidation is the loss of electrons, with an increase in oxidation number. Elemental carbon has an oxidation number of 0, and carbon has an oxidation number of +4 in carbon dioxide, so carbon loses electrons when elemental carbon is converted to carbon dioxide.

Question 7

Choice (B) is the correct answer. When an acid is added to a base, neutralization occurs (e.g., $H^+(aq) + OH^-(aq) \rightarrow H_2O(l)$).

Question 8

Choice (A) is the correct answer. NaCl is ionic, but CH_3OH, CCl_4, CO_2, and CH_4 are covalent molecules. CCl_4, CO_2, and CH_4 are symmetrical, and the bond dipoles cancel, so the molecules are nonpolar. The bond dipoles in CH_3OH do not cancel, so the molecule is polar.

Question 9

Choice (C) is the correct answer. CH_3OH, CCl_4, CO_2, and CH_4 are covalent molecules. The CO_2 molecule is symmetrical, and the central C atom does not have any nonbonding pairs of electrons around it, so the molecule is linear.

Question 10

Choice (D) is the correct answer. Na and Cl are on opposite sides of the periodic table, and the difference in electronegativity is large, so NaCl is ionic.

Question 11

Choice (C) is the correct answer. The oxides of several nonmetals can form weakly acidic solutions. Carbon dioxide reacts with water to form carbonic acid, H_2CO_3, which is a weak acid.

Question 12

Choice (B) is the correct answer. CCl_4, CO_2, and CH_4 are nonpolar covalent molecules. CCl_4 is a liquid at room temperature and 1 atm, but CO_2 and CH_4 are gases.

Question 13

Choice (D) is the correct answer. A noble gas has completely filled valence orbitals (ns^2np^6).

Question 14

Choice (E) is the correct answer. Ionization energy generally increases from left to right across a period of the periodic table and decreases going down a group. Option (A) represents N, option (B) represents O, option (C) represents F, option (D) represents Ne, and option (E) represents Na. Of the options given, Na is leftmost and lowermost on the periodic table.

Question 15

Choice (C) is the correct answer. Option (A) represents N, option (B) represents O, option (C) represents F, option (D) represents Ne, and option (E) represents Na. Atoms of elements in the halogen group tend to gain one electron easily, forming ions with a −1 charge. When an F atom gains one electron, it has a valence electron configuration of $2s_2 2p^6$.

Question 16

Choice (E) is the correct answer. Option (A) represents N, option (B) represents O, option (C) represents F, option (D) represents Ne, and option (E) represents Na. Atoms lose electrons when they become oxidized. Alkali metal atoms tend to lose one electron easily, forming ions with a +1 charge. When an Na atom loses an electron, it has a valence electron configuration of $2s_2 2p^6$.

Question 17

Choice (C) is the correct answer. Because pH = −log[H⁺], the pH of a solution with H⁺ = 1.0×10^{-7} M is equal to 7.

Question 18

Choice (B) is the correct answer. HNO_3 is a strong acid, so [H⁺] in a 0.1 M solution of HNO_3 is 0.1 M. Because pH = −log[H⁺], the pH of a solution with [H⁺] = 0.1 M is 1. The volume of the solution is irrelevant.

Question 19

Choice (D) is the correct answer. NaOH is a strong base, so it dissociates completely in water. Because pOH = −log[OH⁻], the pOH of a solution with OH⁻ = 1.0×10^{-5} M is equal to 5, and pH = 14 − pOH = 9, which is between 7 and 10.

Question 20

Choice (C) is the correct answer. Acid rain is formed when certain nonmetal oxides, such as SO2, dissolve in and react with rainwater to produce H⁺(aq) ions.

Question 21

Choice (A) is the correct answer. Chlorofluorocarbons, such as CCl_2F_2, break apart in the stratosphere. Some of the species formed act as catalysts in reactions that result in the destruction of ozone molecules.

Question 22

Choice (B) is the correct answer. A metal can be thought of as an array of cations in a sea of delocalized valence electrons. Because the valence electrons are relatively free to move, this results in high conductivity.

Question 23

Choice (E) is the correct answer. Diamond has covalent network bonding. Each carbon atom is bonded to four other carbon atoms with relatively strong covalent bonds, resulting in a hard substance.

Question 24

Choice (D) is the correct answer. An aluminum atom has three valence electrons, a phosphorus atom has five valence electrons, an oxygen atom has six valence electrons, a fluorine atom has seven valence electrons ($2s^2 2p^5$), and a carbon atom has four valence electrons.

Question 25

Choice (C) is the correct answer. In the NCl_3 molecule, N is the central atom. The NCl_3 molecule has 26 valence electrons. Option (C) is the only option with N as the central atom, 26 valence electrons, and an octet of electrons around each atom.

Question 26

Choice (E) is the correct answer. A 0.60 g sample of acetic acid is 0.010 mol of acetic acid. A 0.010 mol sample in 1 L of solution results in a 0.010 M solution.

Question 27

Choice (E) is the correct answer. The elements in the periodic table are arranged by increasing atomic number.

Question 28

Choice (E) is the correct answer. Option (E) is the only option in which the same two elements are combined in two different ratios. In option (D), the ratio is the same (1:2 = 2:4).

Question 29

Choice (A) is the correct answer. There are two sodium atoms on the left side of the equation and one on the right side, so a coefficient of 2 should be put in front of the NaCl. To balance Cl, a 2 should be put in front of HCl. This results in a balanced equation, and the coefficient of H_2O is 1. The final balanced equation is Na_2CO_3 + 2 HCl → 2 NaCl + H_2O + CO_2.

Question 30

Choice (B) is the correct answer. Both components of the solution are liquids. In distillation, the solution is boiled and the component with the lower boiling point vaporizes first and is collected and condensed. Solids, not liquids, sublime. Neither component would crystallize out of solution. Neither component is a solid that can be filtered. Paper chromatography is used to separate colored components of a mixture.

Question 31

Choice (D) is the correct answer. NaOH dissociates completely, so the concentration of Na^+ in the original solution is $1.0\ M$. When the volume of the solution is doubled by adding distilled water, the concentration of Na^+ is halved, so the final concentration of Na^+ would be $0.50\ M$.

Question 32

Choice (E) is the correct answer. According to the ideal gas law, $PV = nRT$. $\dfrac{P_1 V_1}{n_1 T_1} = \dfrac{P_2 V_2}{n_2 T_2}$, and at equal volumes, pressures, and temperatures, $n_1 = n_2$ (the number of moles of gas particles in the two samples are equal). A given number of moles of two different ideal gases do not need to have the same mass, number of neutrons, number of electrons, or density.

Question 33

Choice (C) is the correct answer. The K_c expression is the product of the molar concentration of each gaseous product raised to a power equal to its coefficient in the balanced chemical equation divided by the product of the molar concentration of each gaseous reactant raised to a power equal to its coefficient.

Question 34

Choice (A) is the correct answer. Because the highest occupied principal energy level increases going down a group of the periodic table, atomic radius increases going down each group. Oxidizing agents easily gain electrons. Fluorine most easily gains electrons, so strength as an oxidizing agent decreases going down the group. Fluorine has the highest electronegativity; electronegativity decreases going down the group because the valence electrons are farther from the nucleus. The first ionization energy does not increase but rather decreases going down the group. All of the halogens have the same number of valence electrons (ns^2np^5).

Question 35

Choice (B) is the correct answer. There are two Al atoms on the right side of the equation, so a 2 should be put in front of the $Al(OH)_3$. To balance the sulfate ions, a 3 should be put in front of the H_2SO_4. There are now 18 O atoms on the left side of the equation $((2 \times 3) + (3 \times 4))$ and 12 O atoms in $Al_2(SO_4)_3$, so a 6 should be put in front of the H_2O to balance the O atoms. The equation is balanced, and the coefficient of $Al(OH)_3$ is 2. The final balanced equation is $2\ Al(OH)_3(s) + 3\ H_2SO_4(aq) \rightarrow Al_2(SO_4)_3(aq) + 6\ H_2O(l)$.

Question 36

Choice (A) is the correct answer. According the balanced equation, when 2 mol of $C_8H_{18}(l)$ is consumed, 16 mol of $CO_2(g)$ is produced; $CO_2(g)$ has a molar mass of 44 g/mol, so statement I is correct. When 2 mol of $C_8H_{18}(l)$ is consumed, 18 mol of $H_2O(l)$ is produced, so statement II is not correct. When 25 mol of $O_2(g)$ is consumed, 16 mol of $CO_2(g)$ is produced. When the volumes of the gases are measured at the same temperature and pressure, the volumes are proportional to the number of moles, so statement III is not correct.

Question 37

Choice (B) is the correct answer. A CO molecule has a triple bond. The molecules in the other options have only single bonds. A hydrogen atom can only be bonded by a single bond to another atom.

Question 38

Choice (A) is the correct answer. In the graph, the dashed curve (high temperature) shows more molecules with higher kinetic energies than the solid curve (low temperature). Because KE = 1/2 mv^2 (where m is mass and v is velocity), the average velocity of the gas molecules is higher at the higher temperature. It is a sample of a gas, so the number of molecules does not change when the temperature changes. The number of molecules with a kinetic energy greater than X is greater at the higher temperature. The forces of attraction among molecules are not greater at the higher temperature.

Question 39

Choice (E) is the correct answer. The mass of the $CuSO_4$ hydrate is 37.3 g −12.3 g = 25.0 g. The mass of the $CuSO_4$ is 28.3 g −12.3 g = 16.0 g. This means that the mass of the H_2O driven off was 25.0 g −16.0 g = 9.0 g. Because 1 mol water has a mass of 18 g, 0.50 mol of H_2O was driven off. $CuSO_4$ has a molar mass of 160 g/mol, so 16.0 g of $CuSO_4$ represents 0.10 mol of $CuSO_4$. The number of moles of H_2O is five times the number of moles of $CuSO_4$, so the formula of the hydrate is $CuSO_4 \cdot 5H_2O$.

Question 40

Choice (E) is the correct answer. The product in one case is a colorless gas, and the product in the other case is a brown gas, so the products are different substances. The only variable that was changed was the concentration of the acid, so the product must depend on the concentration of the acid. There is not enough information given to determine whether the other options are true.

Question 41

Choice (D) is the correct answer. Hydrogen bonding occurs between molecules in which H is bonded to F, O, or N. This is not true in B_2H_6 or CH_4 but is true in all the other compounds in the other options.

Question 42

Choice (A) is the correct answer. The pressure is highest in the container with the greatest number of moles of gas. Because the number of moles is equal to the number of grams divided by the molar mass, the number of moles is greatest when the molar mass is lowest. H_2 has the lowest molar mass of the options given.

Question 43

Choice (E) is the correct answer. All of the compounds have the same stoichiometry (one metal ion per carbonate ion). The K_{sp} is equal to the concentration of the metal ion times the concentration of the CO_3^{2-}, so the solution with the smallest K_{sp} has the lowest concentration of CO_3^{2-}.

Question 44

Choice (E) is the correct answer. The balanced chemical equation is $N_2 + O_2 \rightarrow 2\ NO$. A 5.0 mol sample of N_2 can produce a maximum of 10. mol of NO. The molar mass of NO is 30. g/mol, so 10. mol of NO has a mass of 300 g.

Question 45

Choice (B) is the correct answer. The substance starts as a liquid, so XY must represent the solidifying (freezing) of the substance; the temperature does not change during a phase change. W shows the highest temperature during the experiment, but the temperature of the substance could most likely be increased. The freezing point is the temperature along segment XY, not at Z. The temperature is not constant along YZ; rather, it decreases. The freezing point of a substance does not depend on the rate at which the substance cools.

Question 46

Choice (D) is the correct answer. When an ionic solid is dissolved in water, the ions are free to move in the solution and the solution can conduct an electric current. Also, the density increases. When a solute dissolves in water, the boiling point increases, the freezing point decreases, and the vapor pressure decreases.

Question 47

Choice (E) is the correct answer. Because $q = mc\Delta T$ (where q is heat, m is mass, c is specific heat capacity, and ΔT is the change in temperature), the calculation is as follows: $q = 2.0 \text{ g} \times (0.13 \text{ J/(g} \times °C)) \times (35.0°C - 25.0°C)$ = 2.6 J.

Question 48

Choice (C) is the correct answer. There is 0.50 mol of O in 0.50 mol of CO, $4 \times 0.10 \text{ mol} = 0.40$ mol of O in 0.10 mol of H_2SO_4, and $6 \times 0.10 \text{ mol} = 0.60$ mol of O in 0.10 mol of $C_6H_{12}O_6$. A sample containing 3.0×10^6 molecules contains much less than 1 mole. A sample containing 3.0×10^{23} molecules contains 0.50 mol of molecules, and there is 0.50 mol of O in 0.50 mol of H_2O. The largest number of moles of O, and thus the largest mass of O, is in 0.10 mol of $C_6H_{12}O_6$.

Question 49

Choice (B) is the correct answer. The product formed is Al_2S_3. The balanced chemical equation is: $2 \text{ Al} + 3 \text{ S} \rightarrow Al_2S_3$

Question 50

Choice (D) is the correct answer. Because Cd^{2+} has a charge of +2, it takes 2.0 mol of electrons to reduce 1.0 mol of Cd^{2+} to Cd. Because Rh^+ has a charge of +1, 2.0 mol of electrons can reduce 2.0 mol of Rh^+ to Rh.

Question 51

Choice (E) is the correct answer. According to the balanced chemical equation, when 4.0 mol of Al(s) and 3.0 mol of O_2(g) react, the maximum amount of Al_2O_3(s) that can form is 2.0 mol. Therefore, anything equal to or less than 2.0 mol is possible, but 2.5 mol is not possible.

Question 52

Choice (C) is the correct answer. When most metals are added to a strong HCl solution, metal cations (which have "disappeared" in solution) and H_2(g) are produced. A precipitate does not form, and Zn^{2+}(aq) is not colored.

Question 53

Choice (D) is the correct answer. There are four C atoms on the left side of the equation, so a 4 should be put in front of the $CO_2(g)$. There are ten H atoms on the left side of the equation, so a 5 should be put in front of the $H_2O(g)$. This results in 13 O atoms on the right side of the equation, so $\frac{13}{2}$ should be put in front of the $O_2(g)$. The coefficients should all be whole numbers, so all of the coefficients should be multiplied by 2. The coefficient of $CO_2(g)$ is therefore 8. The final balanced equation is $2\ C_4H_{10}(g) + 13\ O_2(g) \rightarrow 8\ CO_2(g) + 10\ H_2O(g)$.

Question 54

Choice (C) is the correct answer. When $HCl(g)$ is bubbled into water, it dissolves and forms $HCl(aq)$, a strong acid that completely ionizes to form $H^+(aq)$ and $Cl^-(aq)$. Thus, the solution has a pH lower than 7. Because $HCl(aq)$ is completely ionized, the solution conducts an electric current. Litmus paper turns blue in a basic solution.

Question 55

Choice (E) is the correct answer. The activation energy is the energy needed for a chemical reaction to occur and is shown on the graph as the difference between the energy of the reactants and the maximum energy plotted. The potential energy of the products is the energy shown by the horizontal part of the plot on the right. The potential energy of the reactants is the energy shown by the horizontal part of the plot on the left. The overall energy of reaction is the difference between the energy of the products and the energy of the reactants.

Question 56

Choice (B) is the correct answer. When an alkali metal, M, is placed in water, the products are $M^+(aq)$, $OH^-(aq)$, and $H_2(g)$. Option (B) gives these products in a balanced chemical equation.

Question 57

Choice (D) is the correct answer. Heat is absorbed when substances sublime, so the sublimation of $CO_2(s)$ is endothermic. Oxidation reactions (e.g., (A) and (B)) are typically exothermic, and heat is released when acids are added to water and also as vapors condense.

Question 58

Choice (C) is the correct answer. Potassium iodide is soluble in water, but iron filings and silica are not. Water can be added to the mixture, and the iron filings and silica can be filtered out. The water can then be evaporated from the potassium iodide solution, leaving solid potassium iodide solid behind.

Question 59

Choice (B) is the correct answer. $PV = nRT$. $\dfrac{P_1 V_1}{T_1} = \dfrac{P_2 V_2}{T_2}$, so $V_2 = \dfrac{P_1 V_1 T_2}{T_1 P_2} = V_1\left(\dfrac{T_2}{T_1}\right)\left(\dfrac{P_1}{P_2}\right)$. The Kelvin temperature should be used. Standard temperature is 273 K (T_2) and standard pressure is 760 mm Hg (P_2).

Question 60

Choice (E) is the correct answer. $BaSO_4$ is very insoluble. Nitrates and chlorides are typically soluble. Specifically, $Ca(NO_3)_2$, $Fe(NO_3)_2$, and $Cu(NO_3)_2$, and $BaCl_2$ are fairly soluble.

Question 61

Choice (D) is the correct answer. For 2 mol of $C_3H_7OH(g)$, a coefficient of 2 should be put in front of the $C_3H_7OH(g)$. This results in six C atoms on the left side of the equation, so a 6 should be put in front of the $CO_2(g)$. There are sixteen H atoms on the left side of the equation, so an 8 should be put in front of the $H_2O(g)$. This results in 20 O atoms on the right side of the equation. There are two O atoms in 2 molecules of $C_3H_7OH(g)$, so 18 O atoms are needed from $O_2(g)$. A coefficient of 9 should be put in front of the $O_2(g)$. The final balanced equation is $2\ C_3H_7OH(g) + 9\ O_2(g) \rightarrow 6\ CO_2(g) + 8\ H_2O(g)$.

Question 62

Choice (E) is the correct answer. None of the oxidation numbers change in the reaction in option (E). The oxidation number of hydrogen is +1 in all species. The oxidation number of oxygen is −2 in the hydroxide ion and in water. Oxidation numbers change in the reactions in all of the other options. The oxidation number of elements is 0 in their elemental forms (e.g., in Cl_2, C, and O_2).

Question 63

Choice (B) is the correct answer. A 1.0 L sample of 0.04 M HCl contains 0.04 mol of HCl. Because 2.0 M HCl contains 2.0 mol of HCl in 1000 mL of solution, there is 0.04 mol of HCl in 20 mL of HCl (0.04 mol × 1000 mL/2.0 mol = 20 mL).

Question 64

Choice (B) is the correct answer. A 1.0 mol sample of a gas at 0°C and 1 atm occupies 22.4 L, so 1.12 L contains $\dfrac{1\ mol}{22.4\ L}$ × 1.12 L = 0.0500 mol. Because 1 mol contains 6.02×10^{23} molecules, 0.0500 mol contains $0.0500\ (6.02 \times 10^{23})$ molecules.

Question 65

Choice (B) is the correct answer. The first ionization energy is the energy required to remove an electron from a gaseous atom. This is represented by equation (B).

Question 66

Choice (D) is the correct answer. The electron configuration of a Cl atom is $1s^2\,2s^2 2p^6\,3s^2 3p^5$. The highest energy orbital occupied by electrons in a Cl atom is therefore the $3p$ orbital.

Question 67

Choice (A) is the correct answer. If oxide XO is 64% oxygen by mass and thus 36% element X by mass, it contains 36 g of element X for every 4.0 mol of O (64 g × 1.0 mol/16 g = 4.0 mol) and, by proportion, 9.0 g of element X for every 1.0 mol of O. Therefore, element X has an atomic mass of 9.0 amu.

Question 68

Choice (A) is the correct answer. At a given temperature, all gases have the same average kinetic energy. Because KE = 1/2 mv^2 (where m is mass and v is speed), v is inversely proportional to the square root of the mass. Thus at a given temperature, gases with molecules that have a lower mass have molecules with a higher average speed. The molecules that move fastest effuse fastest. The option with the gas that has molecules of lowest mass is H_2.

Question 69

Choice (C) is the correct answer. When HX ionizes, equal numbers of H^+ and X^- ions form. Therefore, $K_a = \dfrac{(10^{-3})(10^{-3})}{\sim 0.10} = 10^{-5}$.

Question 70

Choice (D) is the correct answer. There is 18 g of H_2O in 1 mol of H_2O. 13 kJ/g × 18 g = 230 kJ.

Question 101

Choice (T, T, CE) is the correct answer. When $NaHCO_3$ is added to an acid, $HCO_3^-(aq)$ reacts with $H^+(aq)$, neutralizing the acid, and thus functioning as a base. Therefore, both statements are true and the second statement is a correct explanation of the first statement.

Question 102

Choice (F, F) is the correct answer. Going down the alkali metal group of the periodic table, the elements are more reactive (e.g., when they are placed in water, the reaction is more violent), so the first statement is false. Atomic radius increases going down a group of the periodic table, so the second statement is false.

Question 103

Choice (T, T, CE) is the correct answer. The P, V, and T behavior of an ideal gas is described by the ideal gas equation. For the equation to be accurate, attractive and repulsive forces between the molecules of a gas must be negligible and the actual volume of the gas molecules must be negligible compared with the volume of the container. At high temperatures and low pressures, gas molecules are relatively far apart, so the attractive forces between them are very weak. Also, the actual volume of the molecules is small compared with the volume of the container. Gases therefore behave more ideally at high temperatures and low pressures. Both statements are true, and the second statement is a correct explanation of the first statement.

Question 104

Choice (F, T) is the correct answer. Isotopes are atoms of the same element with different numbers of neutrons, not different numbers of protons. Therefore, the first statement is false. Because isotopes of a given element have different numbers of neutrons, they do have different atomic masses, so the second statement is true.

Question 105

Choice (T, T, CE) is the correct answer. When an electron of an atom in an excited state drops down to a lower energy level, a quantized amount of energy is released. This produces a bright-line emission spectrum. Therefore, both statements are true and the second statement is a correct explanation of the first statement.

Question 106

Choice (F, T) is the correct answer. Acetic acid is a weak acid because it only partially ionizes in aqueous solution. A molecule of $HC_2H_3O_2$ contains four hydrogen atoms.

Question 107

Choice (T, F) is the correct answer. Temperature remains constant during a change of state. Gases have more entropy than liquids, so the second statement is false.

Question 108

Choice (T, T, CE) is the correct answer. For the autoionization of water, $K_w = [H_3O^+][OH^-]$. At 25°C, $[H_3O^+] = 10^{-7}$ M and $[OH^-] = 10^{-7}$ M, so $K_w = 10^{-14}$.

Question 109

Choice (T, T, CE) is the correct answer. When water is added to concentrated acid, a large amount of heat is produced and the mixture may splatter. If the acid is added to water, the heat produced as the acid is diluted is absorbed by the relatively large amount of water, so the mixture is much less likely to splatter.

Question 110

Choice (T, T) is the correct answer. The second statement is true because sugar is a solid at room temperature and water is a liquid, thus sugar has a higher melting point than water does. Adding a solute to water increases the boiling point. This property does not depend on the relative melting point of the solute, so the second statement is not a correct explanation of the first statement.

Question 111

Choice (T, F) is the correct answer. When an Na atom loses an electron to form a Na$^+$ ion, its radius decreases. The second statement is therefore false. The process Na(g) $\rightarrow$ Na$^+$(g) + e^- represents the ionization of Na. The electron removed from an Na$^+$ ion is in a lower principal energy level than that of the first electron removed, and it is closer to the nucleus and more strongly attracted to the nucleus. It therefore requires less energy to remove an electron from an Na atom than to remove an electron from an Na$^+$ ion. Thus the first statement is true.

Question 112

Choice (T, T) is the correct answer. C_6H_{14} is a hydrocarbon. Hydrocarbons are flammable because they react rapidly with oxygen to form CO_2 and H_2O. H_2O is not flammable. The mass percent of H in C_6H_{14} is 14 g/(72 g + 14 g) × 100 = 16% and the mass percent of H in H_2O is 2 g/(2 g + 16 g) × 100 = 11%, so the second statement is true. However, the difference in flammability is not related to the mass percent of hydrogen, so the second statement is not a correct explanation of the first statement.

Question 113

Choice (T, T) is the correct answer. The strength of electrostatic attractions between two ions is directly proportional to their charges and inversely proportional to the square of the distance between them. Therefore, smaller ions form stronger attractions than larger ions do. Metal atoms tend to lose electrons to become positive ions, and many nonmetals tend to gain electrons to become negative ions. Both statements are true. However, bond strength is not due to the difference between the tendency of metals and nonmetals to lose electrons, so the second statement is not a correct explanation of the first statement.

Question 114

Choice (T, F) is the correct answer. Gases have more entropy than liquids or solids. There are no gaseous reactants and there is one mole of gaseous product, so the entropy increases as the reaction proceeds.

Question 115

Choice (T, T, CE) is the correct answer. Raising the temperature increases the average kinetic energy of reactant particles, so a greater proportion of collisions occur with enough energy for a reaction to occur (activation energy), and there are also more collisions. This causes the rate of the reaction to increase.

SAT Subject Tests™

COMPLETE MARK ● **EXAMPLES OF INCOMPLETE MARKS**

You must use a No. 2 pencil and marks must be complete. Do not use a mechanical pencil. It is very important that you fill in the entire circle darkly and completely. If you change your response, erase as completely as possible. Incomplete marks or erasures may affect your score.

1 Your Name:
(Print)

Last   First   M.I.

I agree to the conditions on the front and back of the SAT Subject Tests™ book. I also agree with the SAT Test Security and Fairness policies and understand that any violation of these policies will result in score cancellation and may result in reporting of certain violations to law enforcement.

Signature: _____   **Today's Date:** ___ / ___ / ___
                                                                MM   DD   YY

Home Address:
(Print)   Number and Street   City   State/Country   Zip Code

Phone: (   )   **Test Center:** _____
                          (Print)   City   State/Country

2 YOUR NAME

Last Name (First 6 Letters)   First Name (First 4 Letters)   Mid. Init.

3 DATE OF BIRTH

MONTH   DAY   YEAR

Jan, Feb, Mar, Apr, May, Jun, Jul, Aug, Sep, Oct, Nov, Dec

4 REGISTRATION NUMBER

(Copy from Admission Ticket.)

Important: Fill in items 8 and 9 exactly as shown on the back of test book.

8 BOOK CODE
(Copy and grid as on back of test book.)

7 TEST BOOK SERIAL NUMBER
(Copy from front of test book.)

9 BOOK ID
(Copy from back of test book.)

PLEASE MAKE SURE to fill in these fields completely and correctly. If they are not correct, we won't be able to score your test(s)!

5 ZIP CODE

6 TEST CENTER
(Supplied by Test Center Supervisor.)

FOR OFFICIAL USE ONLY
0 1 2 3 4 5 6
0 1 2 3 4 5 6
0 1 2 3 4 5 6

103648-77191 • NS1114C1085 • Printed in U.S.A.

© 2015 The College Board. College Board, SAT, and the acorn logo are registered trademarks of the College Board. SAT Subject Tests is a trademark owned by the College Board.

194415-001   1 2 3 4 5 A B C D E   Printed in the USA   ISD11312

783175

PLEASE DO NOT WRITE IN THIS AREA   **SERIAL #**

You must use a No. 2 pencil and marks must be complete. Do not use a mechanical pencil. It is very important that you fill in the entire circle darkly and completely. If you change your response, erase as completely as possible. Incomplete marks or erasures may affect your score.

- ○ Literature
- ○ Biology E
- ○ Biology M
- ○ Chemistry
- ○ Physics
- ○ Mathematics Level 1
- ○ Mathematics Level 2
- ○ U.S. History
- ○ World History
- ○ French
- ○ German
- ○ Italian
- ○ Latin
- ○ Modern Hebrew
- ○ Spanish
- ○ Chinese Listening
- ○ French Listening
- ○ German Listening
- ○ Japanese Listening
- ○ Korean Listening
- ○ Spanish Listening

Background Questions: ① ② ③ ④ ⑤ ⑥ ⑦ ⑧ ⑨

(Questions 1–100, each with answer options A B C D E)

PLEASE MAKE SURE to fill in these fields completely and correctly. If they are not correct, we won't be able to score your test(s)!

7 TEST BOOK SERIAL NUMBER
(Copy from front of test book.)

8 BOOK CODE
(Copy and grid as on back of test book.)

9 BOOK ID
(Copy from back of test book.)

Quality Assurance Mark

Chemistry *Fill in circle CE only if II is correct explanation of I.

	I	II	CE*		I	II	CE*
101	T F	T F	○	109	T F	T F	○
102	T F	T F	○	110	T F	T F	○
103	T F	T F	○	111	T F	T F	○
104	T F	T F	○	112	T F	T F	○
105	T F	T F	○	113	T F	T F	○
106	T F	T F	○	114	T F	T F	○
107	T F	T F	○	115	T F	T F	○
108	T F	T F	○				

FOR OFFICIAL USE ONLY

R/C	W/S1	FS/S2	CS/S3	WS

CERTIFICATION STATEMENT Copy the statement below and sign your name as you would an official document.

I hereby agree to the conditions set forth online at sat.collegeboard.org and in any paper registration materials given to me and certify that I am the person whose name, address and signature appear on this answer sheet.

Signature _____ Date _____

○ Literature
○ Biology E
○ Biology M
○ Chemistry
○ Physics

○ Mathematics Level 1
○ Mathematics Level 2
○ U.S. History
○ World History
○ French

○ German
○ Italian
○ Latin
○ Modern Hebrew
○ Spanish

○ Chinese Listening
○ French Listening
○ German Listening

○ Japanese Listening
○ Korean Listening
○ Spanish Listening

Background Questions: ① ② ③ ④ ⑤ ⑥ ⑦ ⑧ ⑨

PLEASE MAKE SURE to fill in these fields completely and correctly. If they are not correct, we won't be able to score your test(s)!

1–100: Ⓐ Ⓑ Ⓒ Ⓓ Ⓔ (answer bubbles for questions 1 through 100, arranged in four columns: 1–25, 26–50, 51–75, 76–100)

Quality Assurance Mark ●

7 TEST BOOK SERIAL NUMBER (Copy from front of test book.)
0 1 2 3 4 5 6 7 8 9

8 BOOK CODE (Copy and grid as on back of test book.)
0 A 0
1 B 1
2 C 2
3 D 3
4 E 4
5 F 5
6 G 6
7 H 7
8 I 8
9 J 9
K
L
M
N
O
P
Q
R
S
T
U
V
W
X
Y
Z

9 BOOK ID (Copy from back of test book.)

Chemistry *Fill in circle CE only if II is correct explanation of I.

	I	II	CE*		I	II	CE*
101	Ⓣ Ⓕ	Ⓣ Ⓕ	○	109	Ⓣ Ⓕ	Ⓣ Ⓕ	○
102	Ⓣ Ⓕ	Ⓣ Ⓕ	○	110	Ⓣ Ⓕ	Ⓣ Ⓕ	○
103	Ⓣ Ⓕ	Ⓣ Ⓕ	○	111	Ⓣ Ⓕ	Ⓣ Ⓕ	○
104	Ⓣ Ⓕ	Ⓣ Ⓕ	○	112	Ⓣ Ⓕ	Ⓣ Ⓕ	○
105	Ⓣ Ⓕ	Ⓣ Ⓕ	○	113	Ⓣ Ⓕ	Ⓣ Ⓕ	○
106	Ⓣ Ⓕ	Ⓣ Ⓕ	○	114	Ⓣ Ⓕ	Ⓣ Ⓕ	○
107	Ⓣ Ⓕ	Ⓣ Ⓕ	○	115	Ⓣ Ⓕ	Ⓣ Ⓕ	○
108	Ⓣ Ⓕ	Ⓣ Ⓕ	○				

FOR OFFICIAL USE ONLY				
R/C	W/S1	FS/S2	CS/S3	WS

Page 3

COMPLETE MARK ●	EXAMPLES OF INCOMPLETE MARKS Ⓐ ⊗ ⊖ Ⓓ ● Ⓐ Ⓑ Ⓒ	You must use a No. 2 pencil and marks must be complete. Do not use a mechanical pencil. It is very important that you fill in the entire circle darkly and completely. If you change your response, erase as completely as possible. Incomplete marks or erasures may affect your score.

○ Literature
○ Biology E
○ Biology M
○ Chemistry
○ Physics

○ Mathematics Level 1
○ Mathematics Level 2
○ U.S. History
○ World History
○ French

○ German
○ Italian
○ Latin
○ Modern Hebrew
○ Spanish

○ Chinese Listening
○ French Listening
○ German Listening

○ Japanese Listening
○ Korean Listening
○ Spanish Listening

Background Questions: ① ② ③ ④ ⑤ ⑥ ⑦ ⑧ ⑨

1 Ⓐ Ⓑ Ⓒ Ⓓ Ⓔ   26 Ⓐ Ⓑ Ⓒ Ⓓ Ⓔ   51 Ⓐ Ⓑ Ⓒ Ⓓ Ⓔ   76 Ⓐ Ⓑ Ⓒ Ⓓ Ⓔ
2 Ⓐ Ⓑ Ⓒ Ⓓ Ⓔ   27 Ⓐ Ⓑ Ⓒ Ⓓ Ⓔ   52 Ⓐ Ⓑ Ⓒ Ⓓ Ⓔ   77 Ⓐ Ⓑ Ⓒ Ⓓ Ⓔ
3 Ⓐ Ⓑ Ⓒ Ⓓ Ⓔ   28 Ⓐ Ⓑ Ⓒ Ⓓ Ⓔ   53 Ⓐ Ⓑ Ⓒ Ⓓ Ⓔ   78 Ⓐ Ⓑ Ⓒ Ⓓ Ⓔ
4 Ⓐ Ⓑ Ⓒ Ⓓ Ⓔ   29 Ⓐ Ⓑ Ⓒ Ⓓ Ⓔ   54 Ⓐ Ⓑ Ⓒ Ⓓ Ⓔ   79 Ⓐ Ⓑ Ⓒ Ⓓ Ⓔ
5 Ⓐ Ⓑ Ⓒ Ⓓ Ⓔ   30 Ⓐ Ⓑ Ⓒ Ⓓ Ⓔ   55 Ⓐ Ⓑ Ⓒ Ⓓ Ⓔ   80 Ⓐ Ⓑ Ⓒ Ⓓ Ⓔ
6 Ⓐ Ⓑ Ⓒ Ⓓ Ⓔ   31 Ⓐ Ⓑ Ⓒ Ⓓ Ⓔ   56 Ⓐ Ⓑ Ⓒ Ⓓ Ⓔ   81 Ⓐ Ⓑ Ⓒ Ⓓ Ⓔ
7 Ⓐ Ⓑ Ⓒ Ⓓ Ⓔ   32 Ⓐ Ⓑ Ⓒ Ⓓ Ⓔ   57 Ⓐ Ⓑ Ⓒ Ⓓ Ⓔ   82 Ⓐ Ⓑ Ⓒ Ⓓ Ⓔ
8 Ⓐ Ⓑ Ⓒ Ⓓ Ⓔ   33 Ⓐ Ⓑ Ⓒ Ⓓ Ⓔ   58 Ⓐ Ⓑ Ⓒ Ⓓ Ⓔ   83 Ⓐ Ⓑ Ⓒ Ⓓ Ⓔ
9 Ⓐ Ⓑ Ⓒ Ⓓ Ⓔ   34 Ⓐ Ⓑ Ⓒ Ⓓ Ⓔ   59 Ⓐ Ⓑ Ⓒ Ⓓ Ⓔ   84 Ⓐ Ⓑ Ⓒ Ⓓ Ⓔ
10 Ⓐ Ⓑ Ⓒ Ⓓ Ⓔ   35 Ⓐ Ⓑ Ⓒ Ⓓ Ⓔ   60 Ⓐ Ⓑ Ⓒ Ⓓ Ⓔ   85 Ⓐ Ⓑ Ⓒ Ⓓ Ⓔ
11 Ⓐ Ⓑ Ⓒ Ⓓ Ⓔ   36 Ⓐ Ⓑ Ⓒ Ⓓ Ⓔ   61 Ⓐ Ⓑ Ⓒ Ⓓ Ⓔ   86 Ⓐ Ⓑ Ⓒ Ⓓ Ⓔ
12 Ⓐ Ⓑ Ⓒ Ⓓ Ⓔ   37 Ⓐ Ⓑ Ⓒ Ⓓ Ⓔ   62 Ⓐ Ⓑ Ⓒ Ⓓ Ⓔ   87 Ⓐ Ⓑ Ⓒ Ⓓ Ⓔ
13 Ⓐ Ⓑ Ⓒ Ⓓ Ⓔ   38 Ⓐ Ⓑ Ⓒ Ⓓ Ⓔ   63 Ⓐ Ⓑ Ⓒ Ⓓ Ⓔ   88 Ⓐ Ⓑ Ⓒ Ⓓ Ⓔ
14 Ⓐ Ⓑ Ⓒ Ⓓ Ⓔ   39 Ⓐ Ⓑ Ⓒ Ⓓ Ⓔ   64 Ⓐ Ⓑ Ⓒ Ⓓ Ⓔ   89 Ⓐ Ⓑ Ⓒ Ⓓ Ⓔ
15 Ⓐ Ⓑ Ⓒ Ⓓ Ⓔ   40 Ⓐ Ⓑ Ⓒ Ⓓ Ⓔ   65 Ⓐ Ⓑ Ⓒ Ⓓ Ⓔ   90 Ⓐ Ⓑ Ⓒ Ⓓ Ⓔ
16 Ⓐ Ⓑ Ⓒ Ⓓ Ⓔ   41 Ⓐ Ⓑ Ⓒ Ⓓ Ⓔ   66 Ⓐ Ⓑ Ⓒ Ⓓ Ⓔ   91 Ⓐ Ⓑ Ⓒ Ⓓ Ⓔ
17 Ⓐ Ⓑ Ⓒ Ⓓ Ⓔ   42 Ⓐ Ⓑ Ⓒ Ⓓ Ⓔ   67 Ⓐ Ⓑ Ⓒ Ⓓ Ⓔ   92 Ⓐ Ⓑ Ⓒ Ⓓ Ⓔ
18 Ⓐ Ⓑ Ⓒ Ⓓ Ⓔ   43 Ⓐ Ⓑ Ⓒ Ⓓ Ⓔ   68 Ⓐ Ⓑ Ⓒ Ⓓ Ⓔ   93 Ⓐ Ⓑ Ⓒ Ⓓ Ⓔ
19 Ⓐ Ⓑ Ⓒ Ⓓ Ⓔ   44 Ⓐ Ⓑ Ⓒ Ⓓ Ⓔ   69 Ⓐ Ⓑ Ⓒ Ⓓ Ⓔ   94 Ⓐ Ⓑ Ⓒ Ⓓ Ⓔ
20 Ⓐ Ⓑ Ⓒ Ⓓ Ⓔ   45 Ⓐ Ⓑ Ⓒ Ⓓ Ⓔ   70 Ⓐ Ⓑ Ⓒ Ⓓ Ⓔ   95 Ⓐ Ⓑ Ⓒ Ⓓ Ⓔ
21 Ⓐ Ⓑ Ⓒ Ⓓ Ⓔ   46 Ⓐ Ⓑ Ⓒ Ⓓ Ⓔ   71 Ⓐ Ⓑ Ⓒ Ⓓ Ⓔ   96 Ⓐ Ⓑ Ⓒ Ⓓ Ⓔ
22 Ⓐ Ⓑ Ⓒ Ⓓ Ⓔ   47 Ⓐ Ⓑ Ⓒ Ⓓ Ⓔ   72 Ⓐ Ⓑ Ⓒ Ⓓ Ⓔ   97 Ⓐ Ⓑ Ⓒ Ⓓ Ⓔ
23 Ⓐ Ⓑ Ⓒ Ⓓ Ⓔ   48 Ⓐ Ⓑ Ⓒ Ⓓ Ⓔ   73 Ⓐ Ⓑ Ⓒ Ⓓ Ⓔ   98 Ⓐ Ⓑ Ⓒ Ⓓ Ⓔ
24 Ⓐ Ⓑ Ⓒ Ⓓ Ⓔ   49 Ⓐ Ⓑ Ⓒ Ⓓ Ⓔ   74 Ⓐ Ⓑ Ⓒ Ⓓ Ⓔ   99 Ⓐ Ⓑ Ⓒ Ⓓ Ⓔ
25 Ⓐ Ⓑ Ⓒ Ⓓ Ⓔ   50 Ⓐ Ⓑ Ⓒ Ⓓ Ⓔ   75 Ⓐ Ⓑ Ⓒ Ⓓ Ⓔ   100 Ⓐ Ⓑ Ⓒ Ⓓ Ⓔ

PLEASE MAKE SURE to fill in these fields completely and correctly. If they are not correct, we won't be able to score your test(s)!

7 TEST BOOK SERIAL NUMBER (Copy from front of test book.)

8 BOOK CODE (Copy and grid as on back of test book.)

9 BOOK ID (Copy from back of test book.)

Quality Assurance Mark ●

Chemistry *Fill in circle CE only if II is correct explanation of I.

	I	II	CE*		I	II	CE*
101	Ⓣ Ⓕ	Ⓣ Ⓕ	○	109	Ⓣ Ⓕ	Ⓣ Ⓕ	○
102	Ⓣ Ⓕ	Ⓣ Ⓕ	○	110	Ⓣ Ⓕ	Ⓣ Ⓕ	○
103	Ⓣ Ⓕ	Ⓣ Ⓕ	○	111	Ⓣ Ⓕ	Ⓣ Ⓕ	○
104	Ⓣ Ⓕ	Ⓣ Ⓕ	○	112	Ⓣ Ⓕ	Ⓣ Ⓕ	○
105	Ⓣ Ⓕ	Ⓣ Ⓕ	○	113	Ⓣ Ⓕ	Ⓣ Ⓕ	○
106	Ⓣ Ⓕ	Ⓣ Ⓕ	○	114	Ⓣ Ⓕ	Ⓣ Ⓕ	○
107	Ⓣ Ⓕ	Ⓣ Ⓕ	○	115	Ⓣ Ⓕ	Ⓣ Ⓕ	○
108	Ⓣ Ⓕ	Ⓣ Ⓕ	○				

PLEASE DO NOT WRITE IN THIS AREA   ○○○○○○○○○○○○○○○○○○○○○○○○○○○○○○   **SERIAL #**

SAT Subject Tests™

You must use a No. 2 pencil and marks must be complete. Do not use a mechanical pencil. *It is very important that you fill in the entire circle darkly and completely. If you change your response, erase as completely as possible. Incomplete marks or erasures may affect your score.*

1 Your Name:
(Print)

Last   First   M.I.

I agree to the conditions on the front and back of the SAT Subject Tests™ book. I also agree with the SAT Test Security and Fairness policies and understand that any violation of these policies will result in score cancellation and may result in reporting of certain violations to law enforcement.

Signature: _____

Today's Date: ___/___/___
MM DD YY

Home Address:
(Print)
Number and Street   City   State/Country   Zip Code

Phone: (____) _____

Test Center:
(Print)   City   State/Country

2 YOUR NAME

Last Name (First 6 Letters)   First Name (First 4 Letters)   Mid. Init.

3 DATE OF BIRTH

MONTH	DAY	YEAR
Jan		
Feb		
Mar		
Apr		
May		
Jun		
Jul		
Aug		
Sep		
Oct		
Nov		
Dec		

4 REGISTRATION NUMBER
(Copy from Admission Ticket.)

Important: Fill in items 8 and 9 exactly as shown on the back of test book.

7 TEST BOOK SERIAL NUMBER
(Copy from front of test book.)

8 BOOK CODE
(Copy and grid as on back of test book.)

9 BOOK ID
(Copy from back of test book.)

PLEASE MAKE SURE to fill in these fields completely and correctly. If they are not correct, we won't be able to score your test(s)!

5 ZIP CODE

6 TEST CENTER
(Supplied by Test Center Supervisor.)

FOR OFFICIAL USE ONLY

103648-77191 · NS1114C1085 · Printed in U.S.A.

194415-001   1 2 3 4 5 A B C D E   Printed in the USA   ISD11312   783175

PLEASE DO NOT WRITE IN THIS AREA

CollegeBoard

SERIAL #

COMPLETE MARK ●	EXAMPLES OF INCOMPLETE MARKS	You must use a No. 2 pencil and marks must be complete. Do not use a mechanical pencil. It is very important that you fill in the entire circle darkly and completely. If you change your response, erase as completely as possible. Incomplete marks or erasures may affect your score.

○ Literature ○ Mathematics Level 1 ○ German ○ Chinese Listening ○ Japanese Listening
○ Biology E ○ Mathematics Level 2 ○ Italian ○ French Listening ○ Korean Listening
○ Biology M ○ U.S. History ○ Latin ○ German Listening ○ Spanish Listening
○ Chemistry ○ World History ○ Modern Hebrew
○ Physics ○ French ○ Spanish

Background Questions: ① ② ③ ④ ⑤ ⑥ ⑦ ⑧ ⑨

Answer grid, questions 1–100, each with options (A) (B) (C) (D) (E)

PLEASE MAKE SURE to fill in these fields completely and correctly. If they are not correct, we won't be able to score your test(s)!

7 TEST BOOK SERIAL NUMBER (Copy from front of test book.)
0 1 2 3 4 5 6 7 8 9 grid columns

8 BOOK CODE (Copy and grid as on back of test book.)
Number column 0–9, Letter column A–Z

9 BOOK ID (Copy from back of test book.)

Quality Assurance Mark

Chemistry *Fill in circle CE only if II is correct explanation of I.

	I	II	CE*		I	II	CE*
101	T F	T F	○	109	T F	T F	○
102	T F	T F	○	110	T F	T F	○
103	T F	T F	○	111	T F	T F	○
104	T F	T F	○	112	T F	T F	○
105	T F	T F	○	113	T F	T F	○
106	T F	T F	○	114	T F	T F	○
107	T F	T F	○	115	T F	T F	○
108	T F	T F	○				

FOR OFFICIAL USE ONLY				
R/C	W/S1	FS/S2	CS/S3	WS

CERTIFICATION STATEMENT Copy the statement below and sign your name as you would an official document.

I hereby agree to the conditions set forth online at sat.collegeboard.org and in any paper registration materials given to me and certify that I am the person whose name, address and signature appear on this answer sheet.

_____

_____

_____

_____

Signature _____ Date _____

- ○ Literature
- ○ Biology E
- ○ Biology M
- ○ Chemistry
- ○ Physics

- ○ Mathematics Level 1
- ○ Mathematics Level 2
- ○ U.S. History
- ○ World History
- ○ French

- ○ German
- ○ Italian
- ○ Latin
- ○ Modern Hebrew
- ○ Spanish

- ○ Chinese Listening
- ○ French Listening
- ○ German Listening

- ○ Japanese Listening
- ○ Korean Listening
- ○ Spanish Listening

Background Questions: ① ② ③ ④ ⑤ ⑥ ⑦ ⑧ ⑨

PLEASE MAKE SURE to fill in these fields completely and correctly. If they are not correct, we won't be able to score your test(s)!

Questions 1–100, each with answer options (A) (B) (C) (D) (E)

Quality Assurance Mark ●

7 TEST BOOK SERIAL NUMBER (Copy from front of test book.)
Digits 0–9

8 BOOK CODE (Copy and grid as on back of test book.)
0 A 0 / 1 B 1 / 2 C 2 / 3 D 3 / 4 E 4 / 5 F 5 / 6 G 6 / 7 H 7 / 8 I 8 / 9 J 9 / K L M N O P Q R S T U V W X Y Z

9 BOOK ID (Copy from back of test book.)

Chemistry *Fill in circle CE only if II is correct explanation of I.

	I	II	CE*		I	II	CE*
101	T F	T F		109	T F	T F	
102	T F	T F		110	T F	T F	
103	T F	T F		111	T F	T F	
104	T F	T F	○	112	T F	T F	○
105	T F	T F	○	113	T F	T F	○
106	T F	T F	○	114	T F	T F	○
107	T F	T F	○	115	T F	T F	○
108	T F	T F					

FOR OFFICIAL USE ONLY				
R/C	W/S1	FS/S2	CS/S3	WS

Page 3

○ Literature   ○ Mathematics Level 1   ○ German   ○ Chinese Listening   ○ Japanese Listening
○ Biology E   ○ Mathematics Level 2   ○ Italian   ○ French Listening   ○ Korean Listening
○ Biology M   ○ U.S. History   ○ Latin   ○ German Listening   ○ Spanish Listening
○ Chemistry   ○ World History   ○ Modern Hebrew
○ Physics   ○ French   ○ Spanish

Background Questions: ① ② ③ ④ ⑤ ⑥ ⑦ ⑧ ⑨

PLEASE MAKE SURE to fill in these fields completely and correctly. If they are not correct, we won't be able to score your test(s)!

1 Ⓐ Ⓑ Ⓒ Ⓓ Ⓔ   26 Ⓐ Ⓑ Ⓒ Ⓓ Ⓔ   51 Ⓐ Ⓑ Ⓒ Ⓓ Ⓔ   76 Ⓐ Ⓑ Ⓒ Ⓓ Ⓔ
2 Ⓐ Ⓑ Ⓒ Ⓓ Ⓔ   27 Ⓐ Ⓑ Ⓒ Ⓓ Ⓔ   52 Ⓐ Ⓑ Ⓒ Ⓓ Ⓔ   77 Ⓐ Ⓑ Ⓒ Ⓓ Ⓔ
3 Ⓐ Ⓑ Ⓒ Ⓓ Ⓔ   28 Ⓐ Ⓑ Ⓒ Ⓓ Ⓔ   53 Ⓐ Ⓑ Ⓒ Ⓓ Ⓔ   78 Ⓐ Ⓑ Ⓒ Ⓓ Ⓔ
4 Ⓐ Ⓑ Ⓒ Ⓓ Ⓔ   29 Ⓐ Ⓑ Ⓒ Ⓓ Ⓔ   54 Ⓐ Ⓑ Ⓒ Ⓓ Ⓔ   79 Ⓐ Ⓑ Ⓒ Ⓓ Ⓔ
5 Ⓐ Ⓑ Ⓒ Ⓓ Ⓔ   30 Ⓐ Ⓑ Ⓒ Ⓓ Ⓔ   55 Ⓐ Ⓑ Ⓒ Ⓓ Ⓔ   80 Ⓐ Ⓑ Ⓒ Ⓓ Ⓔ
6 Ⓐ Ⓑ Ⓒ Ⓓ Ⓔ   31 Ⓐ Ⓑ Ⓒ Ⓓ Ⓔ   56 Ⓐ Ⓑ Ⓒ Ⓓ Ⓔ   81 Ⓐ Ⓑ Ⓒ Ⓓ Ⓔ
7 Ⓐ Ⓑ Ⓒ Ⓓ Ⓔ   32 Ⓐ Ⓑ Ⓒ Ⓓ Ⓔ   57 Ⓐ Ⓑ Ⓒ Ⓓ Ⓔ   82 Ⓐ Ⓑ Ⓒ Ⓓ Ⓔ
8 Ⓐ Ⓑ Ⓒ Ⓓ Ⓔ   33 Ⓐ Ⓑ Ⓒ Ⓓ Ⓔ   58 Ⓐ Ⓑ Ⓒ Ⓓ Ⓔ   83 Ⓐ Ⓑ Ⓒ Ⓓ Ⓔ
9 Ⓐ Ⓑ Ⓒ Ⓓ Ⓔ   34 Ⓐ Ⓑ Ⓒ Ⓓ Ⓔ   59 Ⓐ Ⓑ Ⓒ Ⓓ Ⓔ   84 Ⓐ Ⓑ Ⓒ Ⓓ Ⓔ
10 Ⓐ Ⓑ Ⓒ Ⓓ Ⓔ   35 Ⓐ Ⓑ Ⓒ Ⓓ Ⓔ   60 Ⓐ Ⓑ Ⓒ Ⓓ Ⓔ   85 Ⓐ Ⓑ Ⓒ Ⓓ Ⓔ
11 Ⓐ Ⓑ Ⓒ Ⓓ Ⓔ   36 Ⓐ Ⓑ Ⓒ Ⓓ Ⓔ   61 Ⓐ Ⓑ Ⓒ Ⓓ Ⓔ   86 Ⓐ Ⓑ Ⓒ Ⓓ Ⓔ
12 Ⓐ Ⓑ Ⓒ Ⓓ Ⓔ   37 Ⓐ Ⓑ Ⓒ Ⓓ Ⓔ   62 Ⓐ Ⓑ Ⓒ Ⓓ Ⓔ   87 Ⓐ Ⓑ Ⓒ Ⓓ Ⓔ
13 Ⓐ Ⓑ Ⓒ Ⓓ Ⓔ   38 Ⓐ Ⓑ Ⓒ Ⓓ Ⓔ   63 Ⓐ Ⓑ Ⓒ Ⓓ Ⓔ   88 Ⓐ Ⓑ Ⓒ Ⓓ Ⓔ
14 Ⓐ Ⓑ Ⓒ Ⓓ Ⓔ   39 Ⓐ Ⓑ Ⓒ Ⓓ Ⓔ   64 Ⓐ Ⓑ Ⓒ Ⓓ Ⓔ   89 Ⓐ Ⓑ Ⓒ Ⓓ Ⓔ
15 Ⓐ Ⓑ Ⓒ Ⓓ Ⓔ   40 Ⓐ Ⓑ Ⓒ Ⓓ Ⓔ   65 Ⓐ Ⓑ Ⓒ Ⓓ Ⓔ   90 Ⓐ Ⓑ Ⓒ Ⓓ Ⓔ
16 Ⓐ Ⓑ Ⓒ Ⓓ Ⓔ   41 Ⓐ Ⓑ Ⓒ Ⓓ Ⓔ   66 Ⓐ Ⓑ Ⓒ Ⓓ Ⓔ   91 Ⓐ Ⓑ Ⓒ Ⓓ Ⓔ
17 Ⓐ Ⓑ Ⓒ Ⓓ Ⓔ   42 Ⓐ Ⓑ Ⓒ Ⓓ Ⓔ   67 Ⓐ Ⓑ Ⓒ Ⓓ Ⓔ   92 Ⓐ Ⓑ Ⓒ Ⓓ Ⓔ
18 Ⓐ Ⓑ Ⓒ Ⓓ Ⓔ   43 Ⓐ Ⓑ Ⓒ Ⓓ Ⓔ   68 Ⓐ Ⓑ Ⓒ Ⓓ Ⓔ   93 Ⓐ Ⓑ Ⓒ Ⓓ Ⓔ
19 Ⓐ Ⓑ Ⓒ Ⓓ Ⓔ   44 Ⓐ Ⓑ Ⓒ Ⓓ Ⓔ   69 Ⓐ Ⓑ Ⓒ Ⓓ Ⓔ   94 Ⓐ Ⓑ Ⓒ Ⓓ Ⓔ
20 Ⓐ Ⓑ Ⓒ Ⓓ Ⓔ   45 Ⓐ Ⓑ Ⓒ Ⓓ Ⓔ   70 Ⓐ Ⓑ Ⓒ Ⓓ Ⓔ   95 Ⓐ Ⓑ Ⓒ Ⓓ Ⓔ
21 Ⓐ Ⓑ Ⓒ Ⓓ Ⓔ   46 Ⓐ Ⓑ Ⓒ Ⓓ Ⓔ   71 Ⓐ Ⓑ Ⓒ Ⓓ Ⓔ   96 Ⓐ Ⓑ Ⓒ Ⓓ Ⓔ
22 Ⓐ Ⓑ Ⓒ Ⓓ Ⓔ   47 Ⓐ Ⓑ Ⓒ Ⓓ Ⓔ   72 Ⓐ Ⓑ Ⓒ Ⓓ Ⓔ   97 Ⓐ Ⓑ Ⓒ Ⓓ Ⓔ
23 Ⓐ Ⓑ Ⓒ Ⓓ Ⓔ   48 Ⓐ Ⓑ Ⓒ Ⓓ Ⓔ   73 Ⓐ Ⓑ Ⓒ Ⓓ Ⓔ   98 Ⓐ Ⓑ Ⓒ Ⓓ Ⓔ
24 Ⓐ Ⓑ Ⓒ Ⓓ Ⓔ   49 Ⓐ Ⓑ Ⓒ Ⓓ Ⓔ   74 Ⓐ Ⓑ Ⓒ Ⓓ Ⓔ   99 Ⓐ Ⓑ Ⓒ Ⓓ Ⓔ
25 Ⓐ Ⓑ Ⓒ Ⓓ Ⓔ   50 Ⓐ Ⓑ Ⓒ Ⓓ Ⓔ   75 Ⓐ Ⓑ Ⓒ Ⓓ Ⓔ   100 Ⓐ Ⓑ Ⓒ Ⓓ Ⓔ

7 TEST BOOK SERIAL NUMBER (Copy from front of test book.)
0 0 0 0 0 0
1 1 1 1 1 1
2 2 2 2 2 2
3 3 3 3 3 3
4 4 4 4 4 4
5 5 5 5 5 5
6 6 6 6 6 6
7 7 7 7 7 7
8 8 8 8 8 8
9 9 9 9 9 9

8 BOOK CODE (Copy and grid as on back of test book.)
0 Ⓐ 0
1 Ⓑ 1
2 Ⓒ 2
3 Ⓓ 3
4 Ⓔ 4
5 Ⓕ 5
6 Ⓖ 6
7 Ⓗ 7
8 Ⓘ 8
9 Ⓙ 9
Ⓚ
Ⓛ
Ⓜ
Ⓝ
Ⓞ
Ⓟ
Ⓠ
Ⓡ
Ⓢ
Ⓣ
Ⓤ
Ⓥ
Ⓦ
Ⓧ
Ⓨ
Ⓩ

9 BOOK ID (Copy from back of test book.)

Quality Assurance Mark ●

Chemistry *Fill in circle CE only if II is correct explanation of I.

	I	II	CE*		I	II	CE*
101	Ⓣ Ⓕ	Ⓣ Ⓕ	○	109	Ⓣ Ⓕ	Ⓣ Ⓕ	○
102	Ⓣ Ⓕ	Ⓣ Ⓕ	○	110	Ⓣ Ⓕ	Ⓣ Ⓕ	○
103	Ⓣ Ⓕ	Ⓣ Ⓕ	○	111	Ⓣ Ⓕ	Ⓣ Ⓕ	○
104	Ⓣ Ⓕ	Ⓣ Ⓕ	○	112	Ⓣ Ⓕ	Ⓣ Ⓕ	○
105	Ⓣ Ⓕ	Ⓣ Ⓕ	○	113	Ⓣ Ⓕ	Ⓣ Ⓕ	○
106	Ⓣ Ⓕ	Ⓣ Ⓕ	○	114	Ⓣ Ⓕ	Ⓣ Ⓕ	○
107	Ⓣ Ⓕ	Ⓣ Ⓕ	○	115	Ⓣ Ⓕ	Ⓣ Ⓕ	○
108	Ⓣ Ⓕ	Ⓣ Ⓕ	○				

FOR OFFICIAL USE ONLY

R/C	W/S1	FS/S2	CS/S3	WS

PLEASE DO NOT WRITE IN THIS AREA

○○○○○○○○○○○○○○○○○○○○○○○○○○○○○○○○○

SERIAL #

SAT Subject Tests™

COMPLETE MARK ● **EXAMPLES OF INCOMPLETE MARKS** Ⓐ Ⓧ ⊖ Ⓟ ⊜ Ⓖ ⊘ ⓪

You must use a No. 2 pencil and marks must be complete. Do not use a mechanical pencil. It is very important that you fill in the entire circle darkly and completely. If you change your response, erase as completely as possible. Incomplete marks or erasures may affect your score.

1 Your Name:
(Print)

Last ___ First ___ M.I. ___

I agree to the conditions on the front and back of the SAT Subject Tests™ book. I also agree with the SAT Test Security and Fairness policies and understand that any violation of these policies will result in score cancellation and may result in reporting of certain violations to law enforcement.

Signature: ___ Today's Date: __/__/__ MM DD YY

Home Address:
(Print) ___ Number and Street ___ City ___ State/Country ___ Zip Code

Phone: ( ) ___ **Test Center:**
(Print) ___ City ___ State/Country

2 YOUR NAME
Last Name (First 6 Letters) First Name (First 4 Letters) Mid. Init.

3 DATE OF BIRTH
MONTH DAY YEAR
○ Jan ○ Feb ○ Mar ○ Apr ○ May ○ Jun ○ Jul ○ Aug ○ Sep ○ Oct ○ Nov ○ Dec

4 REGISTRATION NUMBER
(Copy from Admission Ticket.)

Important: Fill in items 8 and 9 exactly as shown on the back of test book.

7 TEST BOOK SERIAL NUMBER
(Copy from front of test book.)

8 BOOK CODE
(Copy and grid as on back of test book.)

9 BOOK ID
(Copy from back of test book.)

PLEASE MAKE SURE to fill in these fields completely and correctly. If they are not correct, we won't be able to score your test(s)!

5 ZIP CODE

6 TEST CENTER
(Supplied by Test Center Supervisor.)

FOR OFFICIAL USE ONLY
0 1 2 3 4 5 6
0 1 2 3 4 5 6

103648-77191 • NS1114C1085 • Printed in U.S.A.

194415-001   1 2 3 4 5 A B C D E   Printed in the USA   ISD11312   783175

PLEASE DO NOT WRITE IN THIS AREA ○ CollegeBoard ○○○○○○○○○○○○○○○○○○○○○○○○○ **SERIAL #**

○ Literature
○ Biology E
○ Biology M
○ Chemistry
○ Physics

○ Mathematics Level 1
○ Mathematics Level 2
○ U.S. History
○ World History
○ French

○ German
○ Italian
○ Latin
○ Modern Hebrew
○ Spanish

○ Chinese Listening
○ French Listening
○ German Listening

○ Japanese Listening
○ Korean Listening
○ Spanish Listening

Background Questions: ① ② ③ ④ ⑤ ⑥ ⑦ ⑧ ⑨

1–100 answer grid, each with options (A) (B) (C) (D) (E)

PLEASE MAKE SURE to fill in these fields completely and correctly. If they are not correct, we won't be able to score your test(s)!

8 BOOK CODE (Copy and grid as on back of test book.)

7 TEST BOOK SERIAL NUMBER (Copy from front of test book.)

9 BOOK ID (Copy from back of test book.)

Quality Assurance Mark

Chemistry *Fill in circle CE only if II is correct explanation of I.

	I	II	CE*		I	II	CE*
101	T F	T F	○	109	T F	T F	○
102	T F	T F	○	110	T F	T F	○
103	T F	T F	○	111	T F	T F	○
104	T F	T F	○	112	T F	T F	○
105	T F	T F	○	113	T F	T F	○
106	T F	T F	○	114	T F	T F	○
107	T F	T F	○	115	T F	T F	○
108	T F	T F	○				

FOR OFFICIAL USE ONLY

R/C	W/S1	FS/S2	CS/S3	WS

CERTIFICATION STATEMENT Copy the statement below and sign your name as you would an official document.

Signature _____ Date _____

○ Literature
○ Biology E
○ Biology M
○ Chemistry
○ Physics

○ Mathematics Level 1
○ Mathematics Level 2
○ U.S. History
○ World History
○ French

○ German
○ Italian
○ Latin
○ Modern Hebrew
○ Spanish

○ Chinese Listening
○ French Listening
○ German Listening

○ Japanese Listening
○ Korean Listening
○ Spanish Listening

Background Questions: ① ② ③ ④ ⑤ ⑥ ⑦ ⑧ ⑨

PLEASE MAKE SURE to fill in these fields completely and correctly. If they are not correct, we won't be able to score your test(s)!

1 Ⓐ Ⓑ Ⓒ Ⓓ Ⓔ	26 Ⓐ Ⓑ Ⓒ Ⓓ Ⓔ	51 Ⓐ Ⓑ Ⓒ Ⓓ Ⓔ	76 Ⓐ Ⓑ Ⓒ Ⓓ Ⓔ
2 Ⓐ Ⓑ Ⓒ Ⓓ Ⓔ	27 Ⓐ Ⓑ Ⓒ Ⓓ Ⓔ	52 Ⓐ Ⓑ Ⓒ Ⓓ Ⓔ	77 Ⓐ Ⓑ Ⓒ Ⓓ Ⓔ
3 Ⓐ Ⓑ Ⓒ Ⓓ Ⓔ	28 Ⓐ Ⓑ Ⓒ Ⓓ Ⓔ	53 Ⓐ Ⓑ Ⓒ Ⓓ Ⓔ	78 Ⓐ Ⓑ Ⓒ Ⓓ Ⓔ
4 Ⓐ Ⓑ Ⓒ Ⓓ Ⓔ	29 Ⓐ Ⓑ Ⓒ Ⓓ Ⓔ	54 Ⓐ Ⓑ Ⓒ Ⓓ Ⓔ	79 Ⓐ Ⓑ Ⓒ Ⓓ Ⓔ
5 Ⓐ Ⓑ Ⓒ Ⓓ Ⓔ	30 Ⓐ Ⓑ Ⓒ Ⓓ Ⓔ	55 Ⓐ Ⓑ Ⓒ Ⓓ Ⓔ	80 Ⓐ Ⓑ Ⓒ Ⓓ Ⓔ
6 Ⓐ Ⓑ Ⓒ Ⓓ Ⓔ	31 Ⓐ Ⓑ Ⓒ Ⓓ Ⓔ	56 Ⓐ Ⓑ Ⓒ Ⓓ Ⓔ	81 Ⓐ Ⓑ Ⓒ Ⓓ Ⓔ
7 Ⓐ Ⓑ Ⓒ Ⓓ Ⓔ	32 Ⓐ Ⓑ Ⓒ Ⓓ Ⓔ	57 Ⓐ Ⓑ Ⓒ Ⓓ Ⓔ	82 Ⓐ Ⓑ Ⓒ Ⓓ Ⓔ
8 Ⓐ Ⓑ Ⓒ Ⓓ Ⓔ	33 Ⓐ Ⓑ Ⓒ Ⓓ Ⓔ	58 Ⓐ Ⓑ Ⓒ Ⓓ Ⓔ	83 Ⓐ Ⓑ Ⓒ Ⓓ Ⓔ
9 Ⓐ Ⓑ Ⓒ Ⓓ Ⓔ	34 Ⓐ Ⓑ Ⓒ Ⓓ Ⓔ	59 Ⓐ Ⓑ Ⓒ Ⓓ Ⓔ	84 Ⓐ Ⓑ Ⓒ Ⓓ Ⓔ
10 Ⓐ Ⓑ Ⓒ Ⓓ Ⓔ	35 Ⓐ Ⓑ Ⓒ Ⓓ Ⓔ	60 Ⓐ Ⓑ Ⓒ Ⓓ Ⓔ	85 Ⓐ Ⓑ Ⓒ Ⓓ Ⓔ
11 Ⓐ Ⓑ Ⓒ Ⓓ Ⓔ	36 Ⓐ Ⓑ Ⓒ Ⓓ Ⓔ	61 Ⓐ Ⓑ Ⓒ Ⓓ Ⓔ	86 Ⓐ Ⓑ Ⓒ Ⓓ Ⓔ
12 Ⓐ Ⓑ Ⓒ Ⓓ Ⓔ	37 Ⓐ Ⓑ Ⓒ Ⓓ Ⓔ	62 Ⓐ Ⓑ Ⓒ Ⓓ Ⓔ	87 Ⓐ Ⓑ Ⓒ Ⓓ Ⓔ
13 Ⓐ Ⓑ Ⓒ Ⓓ Ⓔ	38 Ⓐ Ⓑ Ⓒ Ⓓ Ⓔ	63 Ⓐ Ⓑ Ⓒ Ⓓ Ⓔ	88 Ⓐ Ⓑ Ⓒ Ⓓ Ⓔ
14 Ⓐ Ⓑ Ⓒ Ⓓ Ⓔ	39 Ⓐ Ⓑ Ⓒ Ⓓ Ⓔ	64 Ⓐ Ⓑ Ⓒ Ⓓ Ⓔ	89 Ⓐ Ⓑ Ⓒ Ⓓ Ⓔ
15 Ⓐ Ⓑ Ⓒ Ⓓ Ⓔ	40 Ⓐ Ⓑ Ⓒ Ⓓ Ⓔ	65 Ⓐ Ⓑ Ⓒ Ⓓ Ⓔ	90 Ⓐ Ⓑ Ⓒ Ⓓ Ⓔ
16 Ⓐ Ⓑ Ⓒ Ⓓ Ⓔ	41 Ⓐ Ⓑ Ⓒ Ⓓ Ⓔ	66 Ⓐ Ⓑ Ⓒ Ⓓ Ⓔ	91 Ⓐ Ⓑ Ⓒ Ⓓ Ⓔ
17 Ⓐ Ⓑ Ⓒ Ⓓ Ⓔ	42 Ⓐ Ⓑ Ⓒ Ⓓ Ⓔ	67 Ⓐ Ⓑ Ⓒ Ⓓ Ⓔ	92 Ⓐ Ⓑ Ⓒ Ⓓ Ⓔ
18 Ⓐ Ⓑ Ⓒ Ⓓ Ⓔ	43 Ⓐ Ⓑ Ⓒ Ⓓ Ⓔ	68 Ⓐ Ⓑ Ⓒ Ⓓ Ⓔ	93 Ⓐ Ⓑ Ⓒ Ⓓ Ⓔ
19 Ⓐ Ⓑ Ⓒ Ⓓ Ⓔ	44 Ⓐ Ⓑ Ⓒ Ⓓ Ⓔ	69 Ⓐ Ⓑ Ⓒ Ⓓ Ⓔ	94 Ⓐ Ⓑ Ⓒ Ⓓ Ⓔ
20 Ⓐ Ⓑ Ⓒ Ⓓ Ⓔ	45 Ⓐ Ⓑ Ⓒ Ⓓ Ⓔ	70 Ⓐ Ⓑ Ⓒ Ⓓ Ⓔ	95 Ⓐ Ⓑ Ⓒ Ⓓ Ⓔ
21 Ⓐ Ⓑ Ⓒ Ⓓ Ⓔ	46 Ⓐ Ⓑ Ⓒ Ⓓ Ⓔ	71 Ⓐ Ⓑ Ⓒ Ⓓ Ⓔ	96 Ⓐ Ⓑ Ⓒ Ⓓ Ⓔ
22 Ⓐ Ⓑ Ⓒ Ⓓ Ⓔ	47 Ⓐ Ⓑ Ⓒ Ⓓ Ⓔ	72 Ⓐ Ⓑ Ⓒ Ⓓ Ⓔ	97 Ⓐ Ⓑ Ⓒ Ⓓ Ⓔ
23 Ⓐ Ⓑ Ⓒ Ⓓ Ⓔ	48 Ⓐ Ⓑ Ⓒ Ⓓ Ⓔ	73 Ⓐ Ⓑ Ⓒ Ⓓ Ⓔ	98 Ⓐ Ⓑ Ⓒ Ⓓ Ⓔ
24 Ⓐ Ⓑ Ⓒ Ⓓ Ⓔ	49 Ⓐ Ⓑ Ⓒ Ⓓ Ⓔ	74 Ⓐ Ⓑ Ⓒ Ⓓ Ⓔ	99 Ⓐ Ⓑ Ⓒ Ⓓ Ⓔ
25 Ⓐ Ⓑ Ⓒ Ⓓ Ⓔ	50 Ⓐ Ⓑ Ⓒ Ⓓ Ⓔ	75 Ⓐ Ⓑ Ⓒ Ⓓ Ⓔ	100 Ⓐ Ⓑ Ⓒ Ⓓ Ⓔ

Quality Assurance Mark ●

7 TEST BOOK SERIAL NUMBER (Copy from front of test book.)

8 BOOK CODE (Copy and grid as on back of test book.)

9 BOOK ID (Copy from back of test book.)

Chemistry *Fill in circle CE only if II is correct explanation of I.

	I	II	CE*		I	II	CE*
101	Ⓣ Ⓕ	Ⓣ Ⓕ	○	109	Ⓣ Ⓕ	Ⓣ Ⓕ	○
102	Ⓣ Ⓕ	Ⓣ Ⓕ	○	110	Ⓣ Ⓕ	Ⓣ Ⓕ	○
103	Ⓣ Ⓕ	Ⓣ Ⓕ	○	111	Ⓣ Ⓕ	Ⓣ Ⓕ	○
104	Ⓣ Ⓕ	Ⓣ Ⓕ	○	112	Ⓣ Ⓕ	Ⓣ Ⓕ	○
105	Ⓣ Ⓕ	Ⓣ Ⓕ	○	113	Ⓣ Ⓕ	Ⓣ Ⓕ	○
106	Ⓣ Ⓕ	Ⓣ Ⓕ	○	114	Ⓣ Ⓕ	Ⓣ Ⓕ	○
107	Ⓣ Ⓕ	Ⓣ Ⓕ	○	115	Ⓣ Ⓕ	Ⓣ Ⓕ	○
108	Ⓣ Ⓕ	Ⓣ Ⓕ	○				

FOR OFFICIAL USE ONLY				
R/C	W/S1	FS/S2	CS/S3	WS

Page 3

- ○ Literature
- ○ Biology E
- ○ Biology M
- ○ Chemistry
- ○ Physics
- ○ Mathematics Level 1
- ○ Mathematics Level 2
- ○ U.S. History
- ○ World History
- ○ French
- ○ German
- ○ Italian
- ○ Latin
- ○ Modern Hebrew
- ○ Spanish
- ○ Chinese Listening
- ○ French Listening
- ○ German Listening
- ○ Japanese Listening
- ○ Korean Listening
- ○ Spanish Listening

Background Questions: ① ② ③ ④ ⑤ ⑥ ⑦ ⑧ ⑨

PLEASE MAKE SURE to fill in these fields completely and correctly. If they are not correct, we won't be able to score your test(s)!

1–100 answer grid (A B C D E)

	I	II	CE*		I	II	CE*
101	T F	T F	○	109	T F	T F	○
102	T F	T F	○	110	T F	T F	○
103	T F	T F	○	111	T F	T F	○
104	T F	T F	○	112	T F	T F	○
105	T F	T F	○	113	T F	T F	○
106	T F	T F	○	114	T F	T F	○
107	T F	T F	○	115	T F	T F	○
108	T F	T F	○				

Chemistry *Fill in circle CE only if II is correct explanation of I.

7 TEST BOOK SERIAL NUMBER (Copy from front of test book.)

8 BOOK CODE (Copy and grid as on back of test book.)

9 BOOK ID (Copy from back of test book.)

Quality Assurance Mark

FOR OFFICIAL USE ONLY				
R/C	W/S1	FS/S2	CS/S3	WS

Page 4

PLEASE DO NOT WRITE IN THIS AREA

SERIAL #

 **CollegeBoard**

SAT Subject Tests™

COMPLETE MARK ●	EXAMPLES OF INCOMPLETE MARKS Ⓐ ⊗ ⊖ Ⓒ ◔ ⊘ ⊜ ◕	You must use a No. 2 pencil and marks must be complete. Do not use a mechanical pencil. It is very important that you fill in the entire circle darkly and completely. If you change your response, erase as completely as possible. Incomplete marks or erasures may affect your score.

1 Your Name:
(Print)

Last _____ First _____ M.I. _____

I agree to the conditions on the front and back of the SAT Subject Tests™ book. I also agree with the SAT Test Security and Fairness policies and understand that any violation of these policies will result in score cancellation and may result in reporting of certain violations to law enforcement.

Signature: _____ Today's Date: ___/___/___
MM DD YY

Home Address:
(Print) _____ Number and Street _____ City _____ State/Country ___ Zip Code

Phone: (___) _____ **Test Center:** _____
(Print) City _____ State/Country

2 YOUR NAME

Last Name (First 6 Letters) | First Name (First 4 Letters) | Mid. Init.

3 DATE OF BIRTH

MONTH | DAY | YEAR

Jan Feb Mar Apr May Jun Jul Aug Sep Oct Nov Dec

4 REGISTRATION NUMBER

(Copy from Admission Ticket.)

Important: Fill in items 8 and 9 exactly as shown on the back of test book.

7 TEST BOOK SERIAL NUMBER

(Copy from front of test book.)

8 BOOK CODE

(Copy and grid as on back of test book.)

5 ZIP CODE

6 TEST CENTER

(Supplied by Test Center Supervisor.)

9 BOOK ID

(Copy from back of test book.)

PLEASE MAKE SURE to fill in these fields completely and correctly. If they are not correct, we won't be able to score your test(s)!

FOR OFFICIAL USE ONLY
0 1 2 3 4 5 6
0 1 2 3 4 5 6
0 1 2 3 4 5 6

103648-77191 • NS1114C1085 • Printed in U.S.A.

194415-001 1 2 3 4 5 A B C D E Printed in the USA ISD11312 783175

PLEASE DO NOT WRITE IN THIS AREA CollegeBoard **SERIAL #**

You must use a No. 2 pencil and marks must be complete. Do not use a mechanical pencil. It is very important that you fill in the entire circle darkly and completely. If you change your response, erase as completely as possible. Incomplete marks or erasures may affect your score.

○ Literature
○ Biology E
○ Biology M
○ Chemistry
○ Physics

○ Mathematics Level 1
○ Mathematics Level 2
○ U.S. History
○ World History
○ French

○ German
○ Italian
○ Latin
○ Modern Hebrew
○ Spanish

○ Chinese Listening
○ French Listening
○ German Listening

○ Japanese Listening
○ Korean Listening
○ Spanish Listening

Background Questions: ① ② ③ ④ ⑤ ⑥ ⑦ ⑧ ⑨

1–100. Ⓐ Ⓑ Ⓒ Ⓓ Ⓔ answer grid (questions 1 through 100)

PLEASE MAKE SURE to fill in these fields completely and correctly. If they are not correct, we won't be able to score your test(s)!

8 BOOK CODE (Copy and grid as on back of test book.)
0 A 0
1 B 1
2 C 2
3 D 3
4 E 4
5 F 5
6 G 6
7 H 7
8 I 8
9 J 9
K L M N O P Q R S T U V W X Y Z

7 TEST BOOK SERIAL NUMBER (Copy from front of test book.)
0 0 0 0 0 0
1 1 1 1 1 1
2 2 2 2 2 2
3 3 3 3 3 3
4 4 4 4 4 4
5 5 5 5 5 5
6 6 6 6 6 6
7 7 7 7 7 7
8 8 8 8 8 8
9 9 9 9 9 9

9 BOOK ID (Copy from back of test book.)

Quality Assurance Mark ●

Chemistry *Fill in circle CE only if II is correct explanation of I.

	I	II	CE*		I	II	CE*
101	Ⓣ Ⓕ	Ⓣ Ⓕ	○	109	Ⓣ Ⓕ	Ⓣ Ⓕ	○
102	Ⓣ Ⓕ	Ⓣ Ⓕ	○	110	Ⓣ Ⓕ	Ⓣ Ⓕ	○
103	Ⓣ Ⓕ	Ⓣ Ⓕ	○	111	Ⓣ Ⓕ	Ⓣ Ⓕ	○
104	Ⓣ Ⓕ	Ⓣ Ⓕ	○	112	Ⓣ Ⓕ	Ⓣ Ⓕ	○
105	Ⓣ Ⓕ	Ⓣ Ⓕ	○	113	Ⓣ Ⓕ	Ⓣ Ⓕ	○
106	Ⓣ Ⓕ	Ⓣ Ⓕ	○	114	Ⓣ Ⓕ	Ⓣ Ⓕ	○
107	Ⓣ Ⓕ	Ⓣ Ⓕ	○	115	Ⓣ Ⓕ	Ⓣ Ⓕ	○
108	Ⓣ Ⓕ	Ⓣ Ⓕ	○				

FOR OFFICIAL USE ONLY				
R/C	W/S1	FS/S2	CS/S3	WS

CERTIFICATION STATEMENT Copy the statement below and sign your name as you would an official document.

I hereby agree to the conditions set forth online at sat.collegeboard.org and in any paper registration materials given to me and certify that I am the person whose name, address and signature appear on this answer sheet.

Signature _____ Date _____

| COMPLETE MARK ● | EXAMPLES OF INCOMPLETE MARKS | You must use a No. 2 pencil and marks must be complete. Do not use a mechanical pencil. It is very important that you fill in the entire circle darkly and completely. If you change your response, erase as completely as possible. Incomplete marks or erasures may affect your score. |

- ○ Literature
- ○ Biology E
- ○ Biology M
- ○ Chemistry
- ○ Physics
- ○ Mathematics Level 1
- ○ Mathematics Level 2
- ○ U.S. History
- ○ World History
- ○ French
- ○ German
- ○ Italian
- ○ Latin
- ○ Modern Hebrew
- ○ Spanish
- ○ Chinese Listening
- ○ French Listening
- ○ German Listening
- ○ Japanese Listening
- ○ Korean Listening
- ○ Spanish Listening

Background Questions: ① ② ③ ④ ⑤ ⑥ ⑦ ⑧ ⑨

PLEASE MAKE SURE to fill in these fields completely and correctly. If they are not correct, we won't be able to score your test(s)!

Questions 1–100, answer choices A B C D E

Quality Assurance Mark

7 TEST BOOK SERIAL NUMBER (Copy from front of test book.)
0 1 2 3 4 5 6 7 8 9

8 BOOK CODE (Copy and grid as on back of test book.)
0 A 0
1 B 1
2 C 2
3 D 3
4 E 4
5 F 5
6 G 6
7 H 7
8 I 8
9 J 9
K L M N O P Q R S T U V W X Y Z

9 BOOK ID (Copy from back of test book.)

Chemistry *Fill in circle CE only if II is correct explanation of I.

	I	II	CE*		I	II	CE*
101	T F	T F	○	109	T F	T F	○
102	T F	T F	○	110	T F	T F	○
103	T F	T F	○	111	T F	T F	○
104	T F	T F	○	112	T F	T F	○
105	T F	T F	○	113	T F	T F	○
106	T F	T F	○	114	T F	T F	○
107	T F	T F	○	115	T F	T F	○
108	T F	T F	○				

FOR OFFICIAL USE ONLY				
R/C	W/S1	FS/S2	CS/S3	WS

○ Literature
○ Biology E
○ Biology M
○ Chemistry
○ Physics

○ Mathematics Level 1
○ Mathematics Level 2
○ U.S. History
○ World History
○ French

○ German
○ Italian
○ Latin
○ Modern Hebrew
○ Spanish

○ Chinese Listening
○ French Listening
○ German Listening

○ Japanese Listening
○ Korean Listening
○ Spanish Listening

Background Questions: ① ② ③ ④ ⑤ ⑥ ⑦ ⑧ ⑨

PLEASE MAKE SURE to fill in these fields completely and correctly. If they are not correct, we won't be able to score your test(s)!

1 Ⓐ Ⓑ Ⓒ Ⓓ Ⓔ   26 Ⓐ Ⓑ Ⓒ Ⓓ Ⓔ   51 Ⓐ Ⓑ Ⓒ Ⓓ Ⓔ   76 Ⓐ Ⓑ Ⓒ Ⓓ Ⓔ
2 Ⓐ Ⓑ Ⓒ Ⓓ Ⓔ   27 Ⓐ Ⓑ Ⓒ Ⓓ Ⓔ   52 Ⓐ Ⓑ Ⓒ Ⓓ Ⓔ   77 Ⓐ Ⓑ Ⓒ Ⓓ Ⓔ
3 Ⓐ Ⓑ Ⓒ Ⓓ Ⓔ   28 Ⓐ Ⓑ Ⓒ Ⓓ Ⓔ   53 Ⓐ Ⓑ Ⓒ Ⓓ Ⓔ   78 Ⓐ Ⓑ Ⓒ Ⓓ Ⓔ
4 Ⓐ Ⓑ Ⓒ Ⓓ Ⓔ   29 Ⓐ Ⓑ Ⓒ Ⓓ Ⓔ   54 Ⓐ Ⓑ Ⓒ Ⓓ Ⓔ   79 Ⓐ Ⓑ Ⓒ Ⓓ Ⓔ
5 Ⓐ Ⓑ Ⓒ Ⓓ Ⓔ   30 Ⓐ Ⓑ Ⓒ Ⓓ Ⓔ   55 Ⓐ Ⓑ Ⓒ Ⓓ Ⓔ   80 Ⓐ Ⓑ Ⓒ Ⓓ Ⓔ
6 Ⓐ Ⓑ Ⓒ Ⓓ Ⓔ   31 Ⓐ Ⓑ Ⓒ Ⓓ Ⓔ   56 Ⓐ Ⓑ Ⓒ Ⓓ Ⓔ   81 Ⓐ Ⓑ Ⓒ Ⓓ Ⓔ
7 Ⓐ Ⓑ Ⓒ Ⓓ Ⓔ   32 Ⓐ Ⓑ Ⓒ Ⓓ Ⓔ   57 Ⓐ Ⓑ Ⓒ Ⓓ Ⓔ   82 Ⓐ Ⓑ Ⓒ Ⓓ Ⓔ
8 Ⓐ Ⓑ Ⓒ Ⓓ Ⓔ   33 Ⓐ Ⓑ Ⓒ Ⓓ Ⓔ   58 Ⓐ Ⓑ Ⓒ Ⓓ Ⓔ   83 Ⓐ Ⓑ Ⓒ Ⓓ Ⓔ
9 Ⓐ Ⓑ Ⓒ Ⓓ Ⓔ   34 Ⓐ Ⓑ Ⓒ Ⓓ Ⓔ   59 Ⓐ Ⓑ Ⓒ Ⓓ Ⓔ   84 Ⓐ Ⓑ Ⓒ Ⓓ Ⓔ
10 Ⓐ Ⓑ Ⓒ Ⓓ Ⓔ 35 Ⓐ Ⓑ Ⓒ Ⓓ Ⓔ   60 Ⓐ Ⓑ Ⓒ Ⓓ Ⓔ   85 Ⓐ Ⓑ Ⓒ Ⓓ Ⓔ
11 Ⓐ Ⓑ Ⓒ Ⓓ Ⓔ 36 Ⓐ Ⓑ Ⓒ Ⓓ Ⓔ   61 Ⓐ Ⓑ Ⓒ Ⓓ Ⓔ   86 Ⓐ Ⓑ Ⓒ Ⓓ Ⓔ
12 Ⓐ Ⓑ Ⓒ Ⓓ Ⓔ 37 Ⓐ Ⓑ Ⓒ Ⓓ Ⓔ   62 Ⓐ Ⓑ Ⓒ Ⓓ Ⓔ   87 Ⓐ Ⓑ Ⓒ Ⓓ Ⓔ
13 Ⓐ Ⓑ Ⓒ Ⓓ Ⓔ 38 Ⓐ Ⓑ Ⓒ Ⓓ Ⓔ   63 Ⓐ Ⓑ Ⓒ Ⓓ Ⓔ   88 Ⓐ Ⓑ Ⓒ Ⓓ Ⓔ
14 Ⓐ Ⓑ Ⓒ Ⓓ Ⓔ 39 Ⓐ Ⓑ Ⓒ Ⓓ Ⓔ   64 Ⓐ Ⓑ Ⓒ Ⓓ Ⓔ   89 Ⓐ Ⓑ Ⓒ Ⓓ Ⓔ
15 Ⓐ Ⓑ Ⓒ Ⓓ Ⓔ 40 Ⓐ Ⓑ Ⓒ Ⓓ Ⓔ   65 Ⓐ Ⓑ Ⓒ Ⓓ Ⓔ   90 Ⓐ Ⓑ Ⓒ Ⓓ Ⓔ
16 Ⓐ Ⓑ Ⓒ Ⓓ Ⓔ 41 Ⓐ Ⓑ Ⓒ Ⓓ Ⓔ   66 Ⓐ Ⓑ Ⓒ Ⓓ Ⓔ   91 Ⓐ Ⓑ Ⓒ Ⓓ Ⓔ
17 Ⓐ Ⓑ Ⓒ Ⓓ Ⓔ 42 Ⓐ Ⓑ Ⓒ Ⓓ Ⓔ   67 Ⓐ Ⓑ Ⓒ Ⓓ Ⓔ   92 Ⓐ Ⓑ Ⓒ Ⓓ Ⓔ
18 Ⓐ Ⓑ Ⓒ Ⓓ Ⓔ 43 Ⓐ Ⓑ Ⓒ Ⓓ Ⓔ   68 Ⓐ Ⓑ Ⓒ Ⓓ Ⓔ   93 Ⓐ Ⓑ Ⓒ Ⓓ Ⓔ
19 Ⓐ Ⓑ Ⓒ Ⓓ Ⓔ 44 Ⓐ Ⓑ Ⓒ Ⓓ Ⓔ   69 Ⓐ Ⓑ Ⓒ Ⓓ Ⓔ   94 Ⓐ Ⓑ Ⓒ Ⓓ Ⓔ
20 Ⓐ Ⓑ Ⓒ Ⓓ Ⓔ 45 Ⓐ Ⓑ Ⓒ Ⓓ Ⓔ   70 Ⓐ Ⓑ Ⓒ Ⓓ Ⓔ   95 Ⓐ Ⓑ Ⓒ Ⓓ Ⓔ
21 Ⓐ Ⓑ Ⓒ Ⓓ Ⓔ 46 Ⓐ Ⓑ Ⓒ Ⓓ Ⓔ   71 Ⓐ Ⓑ Ⓒ Ⓓ Ⓔ   96 Ⓐ Ⓑ Ⓒ Ⓓ Ⓔ
22 Ⓐ Ⓑ Ⓒ Ⓓ Ⓔ 47 Ⓐ Ⓑ Ⓒ Ⓓ Ⓔ   72 Ⓐ Ⓑ Ⓒ Ⓓ Ⓔ   97 Ⓐ Ⓑ Ⓒ Ⓓ Ⓔ
23 Ⓐ Ⓑ Ⓒ Ⓓ Ⓔ 48 Ⓐ Ⓑ Ⓒ Ⓓ Ⓔ   73 Ⓐ Ⓑ Ⓒ Ⓓ Ⓔ   98 Ⓐ Ⓑ Ⓒ Ⓓ Ⓔ
24 Ⓐ Ⓑ Ⓒ Ⓓ Ⓔ 49 Ⓐ Ⓑ Ⓒ Ⓓ Ⓔ   74 Ⓐ Ⓑ Ⓒ Ⓓ Ⓔ   99 Ⓐ Ⓑ Ⓒ Ⓓ Ⓔ
25 Ⓐ Ⓑ Ⓒ Ⓓ Ⓔ 50 Ⓐ Ⓑ Ⓒ Ⓓ Ⓔ   75 Ⓐ Ⓑ Ⓒ Ⓓ Ⓔ 100 Ⓐ Ⓑ Ⓒ Ⓓ Ⓔ

8 BOOK CODE (Copy and grid as on back of test book.)

0 Ⓐ 0
1 Ⓑ 1
2 Ⓒ 2
3 Ⓓ 3
4 Ⓔ 4
5 Ⓕ 5
6 Ⓖ 6
7 Ⓗ 7
8 Ⓘ 8
9 Ⓙ 9
Ⓚ
Ⓛ
Ⓜ
Ⓝ
Ⓞ
Ⓟ
Ⓠ
Ⓡ
Ⓢ
Ⓣ
Ⓤ
Ⓥ
Ⓦ
Ⓧ
Ⓨ
Ⓩ

7 TEST BOOK SERIAL NUMBER (Copy from front of test book.)

0 0 0 0 0 0
1 1 1 1 1 1
2 2 2 2 2 2
3 3 3 3 3 3
4 4 4 4 4 4
5 5 5 5 5 5
6 6 6 6 6 6
7 7 7 7 7 7
8 8 8 8 8 8
9 9 9 9 9 9

9 BOOK ID (Copy from back of test book.)

● Quality Assurance Mark

Chemistry *Fill in circle CE only if II is correct explanation of I.

	I	II	CE*		I	II	CE*
101	Ⓣ Ⓕ	Ⓣ Ⓕ	○	109	Ⓣ Ⓕ	Ⓣ Ⓕ	○
102	Ⓣ Ⓕ	Ⓣ Ⓕ	○	110	Ⓣ Ⓕ	Ⓣ Ⓕ	○
103	Ⓣ Ⓕ	Ⓣ Ⓕ	○	111	Ⓣ Ⓕ	Ⓣ Ⓕ	○
104	Ⓣ Ⓕ	Ⓣ Ⓕ	○	112	Ⓣ Ⓕ	Ⓣ Ⓕ	○
105	Ⓣ Ⓕ	Ⓣ Ⓕ	○	113	Ⓣ Ⓕ	Ⓣ Ⓕ	○
106	Ⓣ Ⓕ	Ⓣ Ⓕ	○	114	Ⓣ Ⓕ	Ⓣ Ⓕ	○
107	Ⓣ Ⓕ	Ⓣ Ⓕ	○	115	Ⓣ Ⓕ	Ⓣ Ⓕ	○
108	Ⓣ Ⓕ	Ⓣ Ⓕ	○				

FOR OFFICIAL USE ONLY				
R/C	W/S1	FS/S2	CS/S3	WS

PLEASE DO NOT WRITE IN THIS AREA

◻ ○

SERIAL #

Show up ready on test day.

There are over 25 videos to watch covering lots of chemistry topics. These lessons are great refreshers to help you get ready for the Chemistry Subject Test. And, you can also access video lesson playlists for Biology and Physics.

Disclaimer: Playlists were created based on videos available on Khan Academy. The contents are subject to change in the future.

Want **free** online lessons from Khan Academy®?
Check out **satsubjecttests.org/chemistry**.